Praise for 1st Timer

Get your first-time leadership role on the right foot with this excellent guide from Assegid Habtewold! With the latest leadership insights and tools and tips to make a smooth transition, you can feel confident moving into your new leadership role. A must read!

> **Marshall Goldsmith**, New York Times
> #1 bestselling author of Triggers, Mojo, and
> What Got You Here Won't Get You There

Dr. Assegid Habtewold does a fine job adding his voice to the conversation about emerging leadership and the 1st timer syndrome by covering the key concepts needed for success.

> **Eddie Turner**, Preeminent Authority on Emerging
> Leaders (Forbes) and #6 Ranked Motivational Speaker in
> the World on the 2021 Global Gurus Top 30 Rankings

Whether you're a first-time or a seasoned leader struggling with 1st timer syndrome, this book will give you the practical tools you can use to find your intrinsic value and create even more value for those you lead.

> **Dr. David Burkus,** Thinker50 ranked thought
> leader and author of Leading From Anywhere

This book gets right to the source of what emerging leaders need to know and understand about leadership, and helps guide them to the next level of leadership success. It also establishes Dr. AZ as a true thought leader on this critical subject.

Mark Levin, CAE CSP, 2020-2021 President, National Speakers Association-DC Chapter

At Per Scholas, we often say that talent is ubiquitous; the opportunity to succeed is not. "Overcoming 1st Timer Syndrome" is a good book I plan to recommend for our learners entering their initial technology career position. Per Scholas prepares highly motivated students throughout our nationwide campuses with technology skills training and professional development, many of them experiencing the corporate environment for the first time. Dr. Habtewold offers helpful tips to move past feelings of imposter syndrome that often show up in those early years as emerging leaders.

Ken Walker, Executive Vice President, Diversity & Operational Excellence, Per Scholas

Dr. Assegid Habtewold provides real-world, how-to tips, tools, and strategies for emerging leaders to improve their everyday interactions and leadership abilities. His book is a must-read for those just beginning their leadership journey as well as established leaders. I've known Dr. Habetwold for over 20 years; when it comes to advice and solutions on leadership challenges, he is my go-to source!

Arnold Sanow, MBA, CSP, Author of Get Along with Anyone, Anytime, Anywhere and Leadership in Trying Times

This book is a must for any emerging leader. It teaches you a lot more than how to overcome first-time leadership pitfalls. The book empowers you to make a smooth transition and then thrive as an emerging leader. You will get great insights and practical approaches to succeed in your first-time leadership role and beyond. You have to read this book!

Asmamaw A. Mengistie, PhD, President - American College of Technology (ACT)

Some say that experience is an outstanding teacher. While that may be true, many continue to make the same mistakes, failing to understand how to put what they have learned into action. In Overcoming 1st Timer Syndrome, Dr. Habtewold, borrowing from research and experience, shares practical insights that, if applied, will help emerging leaders achieve success while minimizing mistakes. This is a book I would have loved to have read when I first started leading. I will make sure my children read it.

Dr. Eugene Wilson, President, Texas Bible College

AZ's Overcoming 1st Timer Syndrome is a concise and constructive companion for first-time leaders as they take on new roles and responsibilities. The ideas in this book will help to shape a leadership mindset. And the practical tools and tips will help first-time leaders navigate common pitfalls. This book will give first-time leaders confidence in taking on their leadership role and accelerate their path to proficiency. It will also serve as a just-in-time resource for when problems arise.

Claudia Escribano, Director of Creative Learning Solutions at Technologies

Every 1ˢᵗ time leader will find extremely valuable suggestions in this book to address a wide variety of leadership challenges and opportunities. Experienced leaders also would benefit from reading this book because it addresses so many of the issues that leaders confront and must address.

Neil E. Grunberg, Ph.D., Leadership scholar and educator

Dr. AZ leverages his medical and leadership training to bring forward a comprehensive and prescriptive narrative for emerging leaders who are uneasy about their new role and seeking a guide. If others around you see a bright light, but you feel like a fraud, this book will help you identify why you may be feeling this way and concrete remedies/cures for your self-doubt. Pick up a copy today and begin your pathway to success.

Catherine Zaranis, Founder and CEO, Perform-Link LLC

"Overcoming 1ˢᵗ Timer Syndrome" is a must-read for every emerging leader who wants to continue being successful, moving beyond what may feel like impossible leadership encounters and hurdles. The book is not only well-researched, but also very practical. Today's new leaders facing complex challenges will find the approach and the practicality of the book very helpful.

Dr. Eyob Mamo, Director at Impact Ethiopia

Dr AZ breaks down areas of leadership into bite size chunks that can help first time leaders develop quickly and seasoned leaders realign their leadership skills to be more effective.

Dr. Michael D. Brumfield,
Founder of Finding Your Identity, LLC

I am thrilled Dr Assegid Habtewold wrote this book with 1st time leaders in mind. The early stage of doing anything is the most fragile phase. I wish Dr. Assegid's book was around when I started leading for the first time. I greatly appreciate the insight packed and friendly tone of this book.

Gabe Hamda, PhD, SPHR, President & CEO,
ICATT Professional Services

In this volume Dr. AZ generously shares his knowledge and lessons learned during his own very distinguished leadership journey. Overcoming 1st Timer Syndrome offers a very practical guide for successfully transitioning into your new leadership role. Let Dr. AZ accompany you on that journey.

Carolyn Ryffel, Intercultural Communication
Coach and Consultant

This book is a must-read for new leaders and managers! Stepping into your first leadership role presents opportunities and the reward for years of hard work. However, it also poses significant and generally unseen challenges. Being well prepared is the best antidote to those challenges. By reading this book and doing the exercises, you will be significantly more prepared and increase your success and that of your organization.

Maureen Metcalf, CEO,
Innovative Leadership Institute

Dr Assegid Habtewold's unrelenting quest to help others become better leaders is admirable. His positivity and wealth of coaching experience shines through. If you're in a first time leadership role, this book can be an invaluable guide and asset, as you navigate the leadership challenges you will inevitably face.

Sylvia Baffour, Author, I Dare You to Care

Without fail, in my many years of work in the professional development field, I have observed first-time leaders make the same mistakes repeatedly. However, in his book, "Overcoming 1st Timer Syndrome," Dr. Assegid Habtewold not only identifies what those mistakes typically are he also provides sound advice for working through each one of them. This book is a must-read if you want to start your leadership journey on the right foot and move through those first few months or even years more effectively.

Christina Eanes, Professional Development
Expert at ChristinaEanes.com

If you are looking for a book for yourself or some of the members of your team who are looking to hit the ground running in a new leadership position and avoid some of the pitfalls that are common - Dr. Habtewold's book is for you! In his book, he outlines 11 "Antidotes" for a condition known as "First-Timers Syndrome" which you may have if you are a new or aspiring leader. That can be a nerve-racking experience but "Dr. AZ" guides you through the process with grace and wisdom along with making it easy to understand for all levels. I would highly recommend this for you or your up-and-coming leadership staff to build your team and deliver results! (…spoiler alert, those are two of the eleven!)

David A. Miles, Ph.D. Founder | Principal,
Dr. Dave Leadership Corporation

Overcoming 1ˢᵗ Timer Syndrome

11 antidotes to thrive beyond first-time leadership pitfalls

DR. ASSEGID HABTEWOLD

*A practical primer to smoothly transitioning
and excelling as an emerging leader*

Success Pathways Press

Web: www.successpws.com

ISBN- 13: 978-1-947524-12-5
ISBN- 10: 1-947524-12-7

Printed in the United States of America

Published August 2021

Email: assegid@successpws.com and assegidh@gmail.com
Tel: (703) 895- 4551

Contents

Acknowledgment

I'm grateful to all of you who helped me to create this book. I am especially thankful to my colleagues Sylvia Baffour, Neil Grunberg, Daryl Green, Catherine Zaranis, Eugene Wilson, and Zina Woolridge, who took their precious time out of their busy schedule to read the manuscript and give me invaluable feedback. Thanks also to my amazing editor, Lisa Messinger. Without the help of all of you, it would never have turned out this well.

Preface

Why I wrote this book

I know what fear can do to you

I wrote this book because I know what it feels like to be afraid. We all have fears of certain things, especially when exposed to them for the first time. As a kid, I remember being terrified of dark places and cemeteries. Today I don't fear them at all. Why? I was afraid because I didn't know enough, but knowledge tends to eliminate mystery.

Everything is scary at first. It is a syndrome we all are familiar with. Think about your first-time experiences of driving, dating, interviewing, and so on. You most probably still remember them vividly. As you increased your knowledge, improved your skills, and practiced, you overcame the first-timer syndrome in each area. You began relaxing, enjoying, and mastering these things with ease.

Likewise, to overcome first-timer syndrome as an emerging leader, you need to increase your leadership knowledge and improve your skills. For the scope of this book, regardless of your age, you're an emerging leader if you are a first-timer team lead, project manager, supervisor, or business owner. This mini-book will help you increase your awareness. It allows you to recognize the symptoms of 1ˢᵗ timer syndrome and audit to see whether or not you have already been manifesting some of these symptoms. In this book, I will also share helpful insights to remove any lingering fears you might have from taking your first-time leadership position. I offer models, tools, strategies, and tactics to develop the most critical competencies that empower you to overcome first-timer syndrome.

According to Merriam-Webster dictionary, a syndrome is **"a set of concurrent things (such as emotions or actions) that usually form an identifiable pattern."** If you've been experiencing a set of emotions, such as nervousness, anxiety, worry, and uncertainty since being placed in your new leadership position, you have been affected by first-timer syndrome. The manifestation of these symptoms can ruin your chance to succeed and make a smooth transition in your first-timer leadership position. That is why I wrote this book. It empowers you to develop the necessary mindset and acquire key skills you need to overcome the first-timer syndrome.

To share my firsthand experience as a first-timer

I also wrote this book to share lessons I learned firsthand from first-timer leadership positions I have taken since the early '90s. I was a first-timer:

- Youth leader in the early 90s,
- Student leader in the late 90s,

- Supervisor in the early 2000s,
- Trainer in 2007, and
- Business owner in 2010.

I wrote this practical book based on my own experience and other first-timers' whom I've helped. Everything I'm going to share with you, I have practiced myself and shared with my audiences, coachees, and mentees. Of course, some of the approaches that worked for me may not resonate with you. That is perfectly fine. You may drop those you don't like and customize others to meet your needs as you transition to your first-timer leadership position.

To share what I gained from books & facilitation

This book also came into existence because I wanted to reveal for first-timers the lessons I gained from reading a variety of management and leadership books over the years. However, I'm not going to weary you with literature reviews. This book isn't written for academics but for practitioners, so I have attempted to be as practical as possible. I have also incorporated many of the insights, tools, strategies, and tactics I shared when I was facilitating workshops and webinars for first-timers in government agencies, corporations, and community organizations, both in the US and Africa.

I'm sharing these lessons and tools because I didn't have a head start when I was a first-timer. I wish I'd had a tool like this book, which is dedicated explicitly to first-timers. Instead I plowed through those leadership roles described above without any guidance or preparation. Looking back, I regret not seeking help or finding growth opportunities, such as books, coaching, or mentoring before and during the first few months of my first-timer positions.

To prevent you from struggling & blaming

The same feelings are also shared by my attendees and the managers I coached. They told me they felt alone in their experience, which prevented them from revealing to others what was going on with them. Some struggled and unsuccessfully tried to hide the symptoms, while others blamed themselves and/or others.

One of my coachees described her first-timer experiences as being like crossing a busy street while blindfolded. Another told me that he regretted the energy and time he had wasted for weeks and even months. Some confessed to hurting their health and relationships as a result of the first-timer syndrome.

To equip managers and mentors of first-timers

I also had conversations with mid-level managers and senior executives who didn't feel adequately prepared to help their first-timers. They had the first-timer syndrome themselves, and thought it would eventually go away, and their emerging leaders would be okay in the end. They didn't know how to shorten the syndrome's lifespan. Now, they do.

To share the results of my informal research

I also wrote this book to make widely available the results of my informal research, which I conducted as I was facilitating workshops and coaching emerging supervisors and managers. I studied what someone can do to prepare and excel as a first-timer team lead, supervisor, manager, or business owner. My investigation revealed that the overwhelming majority of first-timers don't begin their first-time leadership role with the right foot and proper support system.

A note of caution: this isn't your typical book. I won't bombard you with lots of literature and references. To begin with, there isn't much research on first-timer syndrome. But I also wanted this book to be practical and based on my personal experience and the experiences of the first-timers I worked with in my coaching programs, workshops, and webinars. Thus, this book is packaged as a primer to help you make a quick and smooth transition in your new leadership role. It is a practical manual designed to offer you hands-on tools and approaches that you can practice right away. The more you practice what you learn, the quicker first-timer syndrome goes away and the more your confidence is increased. I wanted to give you hands-on tools, strategies, and tactics you could use immediately to overcome the first-timer syndrome. My goal was to empower emerging leaders so quickly that they excel beyond their first-timer leadership role.

If you're interested in digging deep about the concepts I cover in this book, there are many resources out there. Just Google them. However, I will share occasional relevant quotations and books relating to some of the leadership concepts discussed.

Even seasoned leaders experience the syndrome

That said, my informal research also revealed to me an interesting fact. Even seasoned supervisors, managers, and executives experience the syndrome when they are placed in a new position for the first time. Clearly, the transition challenges everyone. It has nothing to do with being young and a junior leader; it isn't the place nor the individual. Every transition is scary and challenging. There are uncertainties, doubts, risks, guesses, and so on whenever anyone takes on a new leadership role.

Below are the stages you may pass through on your leadership journey. Of course, depending on your industry, there may be either a shorter or a more extended version of leadership hierarchies. Most organizations, however, have these three levels of leadership progression:

1. Star employee (high performer),
2. Supervisor,
3. Manager, and
4. Executive

As you transition from being a star employee into a supervisory role because of your high performance, you will face specific challenges. Likewise, when you make a transition from a supervisory role to a managerial position, you will experience different sets of challenges that come from leading from the middle. Of course, when you progress to become an executive, you'll also have transition challenges specific to senior leadership.

Regardless of seniority, most experience first-timer syndrome when placed in a new leadership position, irrespective of the organizational hierarchy. Seasoned leaders, however, are likely to become proactive to mitigate the effects, and may therefore be quicker than junior leaders to shorten the learning curve and lessen the impact.

One or more of the following feelings will be experienced by those suffering from first-timer syndrome:

- Anxiety,
- Confusion,
- Frustration,
- Displacement,
- Stress, and
- Uncertainty.

The science behind why the syndrome exists

In this book you'll also learn the science behind why every leader experiences this syndrome. The mindset, attitude, personality, and many of the skill sets that allowed you to excel as a follower, an employee or a leader in another leadership position won't serve you that well in your new leadership role. In fact, some of them may even sabotage your transition. The challenge is that you may not even be consciously aware of the full extent of the syndrome, so you may continue to think, behave, decide, and act as you used to, expecting to get the same fantastic results you got in your previous team member or leadership role.

What got you here, won't get you there

Marshall Goldsmith, author and American executive leadership coach, said, **'What got you here, won't get you there.'** What brought you this far cannot help you any longer to succeed in a new leadership role. You need a new mindset, the necessary skills, and the right personality to succeed from the get-go. This book will inspire, equip, and empower you to succeed as a first-time team lead, supervisor, manager, or business owner.

A smooth transition to future leadership roles

Reading this book will provide you with a strong foundation as you advance in your leadership. You will appreciate that you read this book as you become a mid-level manager, executive, CEO, and beyond. Whatever you learn and practice here will translate into making your future first-timer roles, no matter how challenging they may be, easier and smoother.

The tips you get from this book will equip you to make a smooth transition from your current role to your next leadership assignment. You will also be given insights, tools, and methods to mentor first-timers in your organization, especially your successors, as you help them make a smooth transition by sharing your experience. Finally, everything you learn here will empower you to succeed in your other endeavors outside of work and business. Let's dive in!

Introduction

Who will benefit from this book?

Everyone will benefit from the book

I firmly believe that everyone is born to lead. Of course, I'm not saying that everyone is born into leadership and becomes a great leader right out of the gate. Becoming a successful leader requires work. One cannot simply assume a leadership role without preparing for it and expect to succeed. Fortunately, everyone has the potential to become a leader, at least in the area of their passion. But we are all expected to release and maximize this potential by developing the right mindset, the necessary skill set, and character.

The 21st Century workplace and marketplace have changed. Everyone is expected to pay their dues regardless of where they are in the organization's hierarchy by taking leadership, at least within their job description. In this era, many organizations have become flat, allowing every team member to create, innovate, and take leadership, even if they are at the bottom of the corporate ladder.

That means if you're reading this book, you're a leader, even if you do not have a formal leadership title. And if you're a leader, you will benefit from this book. The antidotes shared here will empower you to succeed wherever you are today, and in the future when you take your first leadership position.

If you already have a team, you're expected to get along and lead successfully from the get-go. If you stumble right away, your people may complain or even leave your team, and that isn't good news for a first-timer, or for that matter, for any leader. "**A Gallup poll of more than 1 million employed US workers concluded that the No. 1 reason people quit their jobs is a bad boss or immediate supervisor…People leave managers, not companies…in the end, turnover is mostly a manager issue.**" You don't want to have such a reputation, especially right out of the gate.

The primary beneficiaries of this book

While it's true that everyone can benefit from the content of this book, below are the primary beneficiaries:

1. **Recently promoted team leads, supervisors, project managers, and business owners**. This book will enable this group to overcome the first-timer syndrome within a reasonable period.

2. **Those who have been in their current first-timer position for a while.** This book provides help for this group to succeed in their current position. They will gain the latest empowering nuggets to implement

right away to achieve quick results. It will also help them appreciate what they have been doing right and not so right, and the changes they should make to address the latter.

3. **Aspiring first-timers.** Even if you are not in a new leadership position right now and don't belong to one of the above primary beneficiaries, this book will prepare you to take your next leadership position.

4. **Seasoned leaders.** This book is also beneficial to senior leaders who are coaching and mentoring first-timers in their organizations.

As you can see, this book is relevant to every leader, regardless of their position and seniority, though its purpose may differ.

The three focus areas

Admittedly, this book cannot cover everything first-timers need. The focus is on three major mandatory leadership development areas:

1. Mindset,
2. Skill set, and
3. Character set.

These three areas are mandatory to overcoming first-timer syndrome. One needs to have the proper mindset, the necessary skill set, and a solid character set and personality in order to make a smooth transition. In fact, these three leadership development areas are foundational for any leader at any level. As you take on more leadership responsibilities, you need to simultaneously work on these three areas to serve your people and organization with leadership excellence.

This book isn't written for 'managers.'

This book isn't written for those looking for shortcut management tricks to manipulate others. There is a vast difference between 'managing' and leading people. Grace Murray Hopper, US Navy rear admiral and pioneer in computer science, put it beautifully: **"You manage things; you lead people."** This book is written to raise leaders who lead by influencing and setting examples, not through tricks and manipulations.

However, I don't want you to misunderstand me. I'm not one of those experts who attempts to wage war between leaders and managers. As much as we need leaders, we also need managers. Besides, managing is an important aspect of being a leader. All leaders are managers, but not all managers are leaders. A leader cannot be successful without the competencies that enable him/her to manage:

1. Self,
2. Resources,
3. People,
4. Projects, and
5. Change.

Leaders who don't manage their own time, emotions, and problems cannot be influential. They cannot delegate these to others to manage for them. As emerging leaders, they also cannot delegate to others management of their scarce resources, team members, projects, or change. I don't want emerging leaders to say, 'I'm a leader, not a manager!' and neglect development of their management competencies.

Of course, when you advance in your leadership, you might hire (delegate) someone who is great at managing so that you can focus on the functions of leading, some of which are:

- Articulating the mission,
- Clarifying the vision,
- Aligning the people alongside the values of the organization,
- Creating and nurturing coalitions.

The point I'm making is that you should be a leader who is skillful in managing, not manipulating. To help you succeed in your leadership, I will provide some management tips in the above five management areas. But the focus of this book is to equip you to 'become' an impactful leader who leads by example. You cannot ask your people to become better in their attitude, skills, and character without you first doing it. Effective leadership begins with self. No one can lead others successfully without first leading self. If that is your desire, you're in for a special treat.

This book isn't enough

Of course, this book by itself isn't the end. You will certainly find some helpful principles, methods, and approaches that will guide you in your journey as a first-timer. You will also learn about fresh perspectives that inspire, challenge, stretch, and equip you as you lead your people and serve your team and organization with excellence. However, you must practice and continue to monitor and evaluate your progress at the end of the day. What is more, you should also read other books and sign up for relevant programs to complement the teachings of this book.

Goals and objectives

To recap, below are the specific objectives of this book:

1. To help configure/reconfigure the mindset of first-timers, which will allow them to demonstrate the right attitude from the get-go.

2. To equip first-timers with the necessary soft and people skills to lead their team effectively and get along with their managers, peers, internal and external customers, and other key stakeholders.

3. To offer practical tools, models, templates, and approaches first-timers should use to lead their team with excellence from the start.

4. To empower 1ˢᵗ timers to develop the personality they need to overcome the first-timer syndrome with ease.

It is an honor to be part of your journey as you overcome first-timer syndrome. I look forward to hearing your feedback once you have read this book. I am also eagerly looking forward to working with you as you develop yourself to become a great leader and serve your community, team, and organization with leadership excellence. Thank you for allowing me to be part of your life and leadership journey by picking up this book!

Understanding
the 11 Antidotes

Overview on the 11 antidotes

Below are 11 antidotes you need to make a smooth transition in your first leadership position. They facilitate your healing quickly from the syndrome. If you take enough doses of these antidotes, not only will they cure you now, but they will immunize you for your future first-timer leadership positions.

- **Antidote 1** - *Know Your Place* increases your awareness. It provides you areas where you need to improve your self-awareness, tells you what kinds of questions to ask, and where to find them so that you 'know your place' by profoundly knowing yourself, the organization, its people, and key stakeholders.
- **Antidote 2** - *Own Your Place* boosts your confidence level. It equips you to translate your knowledge from the first antidote into a positive attitude, emotions, and bold actions, which in turn increases your self-

confidence to be in charge and ultimately to 'own your place.'

- **Antidote 3** - *Build Your Team* multiplies your efforts exponentially. It enables you to understand how team dynamics work, the team-building model, and approaches that build and transform your team to function like a well-oiled machine.

- **Antidote 4** - *Communicate with Stakeholders Effectively* connects you with others. It assists you in recognizing what it takes to communicate effectively with your supervisor, team members, and other critical stakeholders by understanding their communication preferences, coming up with a communication strategy, and improving your communication competencies.

- **Antidote 5** - *Deliver Quick Results* immediately heightens your productivity. It empowers you to deliver results by setting goals, managing your time and energy, and quickly increasing your and your team's productivity.

- **Antidote 6** - *Make Timely Decisions* encourages you in the face of problems and challenges. It prepares you to make tough and timely decisions, even when you don't have enough time and data to rely on, by understanding the problem-solving model, sources of decision-making, and more.

- **Antidote 7** - *Engage Your People* elevates your influence to the next level. It teaches you how to inspire and engage your people from the get-go by recognizing how motivation works and creating a culture that engages, offers proper appreciation, and employs effective delegation.

- **Antidote 8 -** *Strive for Excellence* magnifies your performance. It educates you to realize the place of excellence, how to manage performance, create and sustain a culture that promotes giving and receiving feedback, and how to deal with poor performers.

- **Antidote 9 -** *Articulate Your Leadership Philosophy* makes you predictable. It introduces you to a critical leadership concept - Leadership Philosophy, and explains why it is essential, how to articulate your philosophy, and how to share it with your key people.

- **Antidote 10 -** *Become Authentic and Credible* enhances your trustworthiness. It shows you the place of authenticity and credibility in leadership, the importance of demonstrating immediate authenticity and credibility, exhibiting consistency, and eagerness to learn.

- **Antidote 11 -** *Develop Yourself and Your People* allows you to tap into your and your peoples' potential. It discusses the significance of leadership growth, how to craft your and your team's development plan, and discusses how to help vulnerable team members.

The flow of the book

i. Antidote 1 – 3:

The first three antidotes are designed to start your first-timer role on the right footing. The first two empower you to increase your self-awareness and self-confidence to overcome anxiety and worries and, in turn, to stop hesitating to lead boldly from the get-go. They are designed to clarify and help you develop the right mindset and attitude from the start. The first two antidotes focus on self-leadership, while the third is essential as you transition from self-leadership to leading others. Building your team is the first antidote to becoming a successful first-timer leader who mobilizes others. The third antidote sensitizes you to have a mindset that believes in teamwork and equips you with some approaches to build your team sooner. You should be convinced that you cannot do anything meaningful and succeed as a first timer if you cannot develop and lead your team successfully and quickly.

ii. **Antidote 4 – 8:**

The next five antidotes equip you to develop certain leadership competencies to effectively fulfill your first-timer leadership responsibilities. They will empower you with the most essential skill set necessary for emerging leaders. As a first-timer, once you lead yourself and build your team to deliver results, you need competencies, such as communicating effectively, making timely decisions, breaking impasses, and attaining excellence. Developing these skills empowers you to increase your productivity to succeed in your first-time leadership role. You can't sustain your first-timer position without delivering results, and these competencies enable you to lead your team to meet its goals.

iii. Antidote 9 – 11:

The last three antidotes are focused on developing your character set, personality, and helping you grow to solidify and sustain the results you have accomplished by working on your mindset and skill set. They equip you to craft and introduce your leadership philosophy, become authentic and credible, and constantly develop yourself and your team. As much as you need the right mindset and skill set to overcome the syndrome, you cannot sustain your success and continue to succeed in your first-timer position without character. You should be authentic, credible, caring, dependable, and a servant leader.

The antidotes are not in order of priority

You may choose to work on the specific antidote(s) you need right away. When you reach those you feel you don't need as much, you might decide to read quickly, but when you get to the antidotes you find more important to your circumstance, you might wish to read more carefully, take notes and answer the questions.

To fully benefit from reading this book:

1. **Take each antidote seriously.** Even if you think you already have enough knowledge about a given

topic, don't allow that to stop you from treating each chapter seriously.

2. **Set the right tone.** Consider the upcoming weeks transformational, because they are. This foundational book is beneficial well beyond your current first-timer position.

3. **Engage throughout the book.** Learning happens in many forms. On top of reading each chapter and answering questions, you should immediately practice what you learn.

4. **Share what you have learned.** The more you share, the more you retain. For instance, share with your peers on your intranet or social media the answers to these questions: What are the three top takeaways from each chapter? What is the one action you will take because you read that particular chapter?

ANTIDOTE 1

Know Your Place

"If you know the enemy and know yourself, you need not fear the results of a hundred battles."

Sun Tzu, Chinese military strategist, author, and philosopher

You might have heard people say 'he/she doesn't know his/her place.' People often use this phrase to belittle someone; to tell them they don't belong there. People sense when we don't know our place of leadership. If we don't prepare well for our first-timer leadership position, some might use this phrase against us. The good news is that they also sense when we do know our first-timer place of leadership and this increases their confidence in us. That is why this chapter will equip you to know your place in the best sense. The more you know your place, the more you will 'own your place', which we will cover in chapter 2.'

Knowledge areas as first-timer

The most urgent antidote you need as a first-timer is knowledge. You need to 'know your place' to overcome the first-timer syndrome. This knowledge will be the foundation to build on as you overcome the syndrome expediently. This knowledge should begin from:

- Knowing who you truly are,
- What it takes to succeed in your first-timer position,
- The people with whom you work, and
- The organization, its history, mission, vision, values, strategies, and culture.

Implications and impacts of what you don't know

What you don't know, you cannot:

- Capitalize on,
- Control, or
- Manage successfully.

What you don't know can also:

- Affect,
- Hurt, and
- Sabotage you, your team, and the organization.

Knowing your place is relevant everywhere

Knowing your place is the first antidote. Other antidotes won't be effective unless you have this one first. It is foundational.

Don't buy into the tempting idea that you already know yourself and your current workplace. Go through this chapter patiently, even if you think you already know yourself reasonably well and have been in the current organization for a very long period. On top of knowing your first-timer position better, as well as the organization, its industry, and all stakeholders, the process of knowing your place makes you a better person and leader. Not only do you succeed in your current position, but you also excel when you are placed in future first-timer positions, whether in your current organization or elsewhere. In addition, what you come to know in this chapter will positively impact your personal life, business, and relationships.

Advantages of knowing your place

Knowing your place adequately:

- Allows you to start your first-timer position on the right footing.
- Paints a positive first impression in the mind of the people you work with.
- Positions you to begin your leadership from high ground.
- Prevents you from too much guessing, inadvertently stepping on other people's toes, crossing red lines, bashing boundaries, and committing various 'sins' and offenses. As actress Toni Collette said, **"The better you know yourself, the better your relationship with the rest of the world."**

Pause and review the above list, and evaluate which of these is true in your case (or in the case of your first-timer you're coaching and mentoring).

Worth investing time to know your place

Regardless of having other great competencies as a leader, you will struggle to make a smooth transition if you stumble as a result of not knowing yourself and your place. However, I have to be honest with you. You may not immediately harvest tangible, quantifiable results. It takes time and effort to begin enjoying the fruits of knowing your place.

The good thing is that once you dealt with symptoms that come because you don't knowing your place, you will know the key questions to ask for future leadership positions in which you are placed. You'll also know where to go to get answers for you and others when you take a first-timer position in the future. Whether you are an aspiring first-timer, have just been placed in your first-timer role, or have been in the position for a while, the time is right to know your place very well. And this chapter will provide you with the necessary insights, strategies, and tactics you can employ to know your place well, which will help overcome first-timer syndrome.

Why is it the very first step for a smooth transition?

This is the first antidote to overcome the feeling of frustration, displacement, stress, uncertainty, and consequences that come with it. 'Knowing your place':

- Takes away any mystery,
- Dissipates 'darkness', and
- Positions you to overcome the syndrome quickly.

Knowing your place is especially critical if you are just being brought in to lead a team in a new organization. Even if you have been in that organization long enough and already know all or some of the people, taking this antidote is foundational to succeed in making a smooth transition.

Where to start?

Once you appreciate why it should be the first antidote, the next question is: Where do you start? The knowing should begin with:

- Knowing yourself,
- Your work environment, and
- Key stakeholders.

Diagnostic questions

Let me ask you a couple of questions to figure out whether you have the symptom of not knowing your place.

- Have you felt that you don't belong in your current leadership position? Have others directly or indirectly expressed that you don't deserve it? Did you believe them?
- Have you felt as if you are a stranger in your first-timer position?
- Have you been feeling misplaced in your current leadership position?

If you have said yes to any of the above questions, you have self-doubt. Questioning yourself reveals the lack of knowing yourself very well. If they promoted you, they must have seen some great things in you. It seems you believed your own and/or others' doubts about what qualifies you to take your first leadership role. If you're feeling misplaced, it shows that you're not yet familiar with your environment. These symptoms call for an antidote. And this chapter immunizes you to develop unshakable self-knowledge and elevated awareness of your immediate work environment.

Learning Objectives

The main goal of this antidote is to help you 'know your place' and be comfortable in your new role. Below are the specific objectives of the chapter:

1. To know yourself and increase your self-awareness.
2. To know the main characteristics of your organization.
3. To know the key facts about your job that are necessary to succeed in the organization.
4. To know the key stakeholders, their needs, and priorities.

1.1. Know yourself & increase your self-awareness

Before we succeed in leading others, we should first manage ourselves. Leadership begins with self. Self-leadership starts with self-awareness and ends with personal mastery. In my book **'Soft Skills That Make or Break Your Success,'** the first soft skill is Increasing self-awareness. I wrote:

"…Leadership is elusive for many because they think that the places where they become better leaders are public arenas as they lead others. Unfortunately, the foundation of impactful leadership is self-leadership.

- Understanding who we are, our strengths, and limitations,
- Conquering our thoughts and regulating our emotions,
- Managing our time and energy,
- Overcoming obstacles and solving problems, and
- Making wise and right decisions and demonstrating a commitment to our decisions are where we learn to lead ourselves first. Without first conquering self, the chance to prevail upon anything else outside over which we don't have control is a huge hurdle, to say the least…"

Thus, to know your first-timer place very well, begin the journey by understanding your 'true self.' I like what Greek philosopher, Thales, said, **"The most difficult thing in life is to know yourself."** The more you know your true self, the more you can see your unique role in the leadership position in which you've been placed and the more you can lead others successfully. Follow the guidelines of Visa Card Association founder Dee Hock: **"If you seek to lead, invest at least 50 percent of your time in leading yourself--your own purpose, ethics,**

principles, motivation, conduct. Invest at least 20 percent leading those with authority over you and 15 percent leading your peers."

Rate your knowing

From 1 to 5, 1 being clueless about who you truly are, and 5 being incredibly self-aware, how do you rate yourself?

If you scored less than 3, you should spend time discovering your true self by asking the following questions:

- Who am I?
- Why am I in this organization?
- What makes me unique?

Many organizations embraced self-awareness

I know it looks like these questions are philosophical and have nothing to do with supervision, management, and leadership. That isn't true anymore. Many corporations now arrange programs to increase the self-awareness of their leaders. They make them take personality tests to know themselves, their strengths, limitations, and uncover their blind spots and recognize their leadership styles. These smart organizations realized that individual self-discovery is the foundation of corporate identity. These organizations also came to appreciate that the more they know their people, and the more their people know themselves, the easier it is to place them where they are passionate and where they can be productive. It is a win-win for both the greater good and individual members.

Knowing that each person in an organization is indispensable in the 21ˢᵗ Century, many organizations encourage their people to contribute toward corporate goals based on their uniqueness and strengths. Trust me. If this theme isn't yet appreciated in your organization, it will soon be relevant in your work or marketplace.

Regardless, recognize that the more you know yourself, the more you know others and the environment and know how you can serve them better. When you know your strengths, you leverage them properly. When you discover your limitations, you become intentional in improving them. The more you uncover your blind spots, the more you will stop sabotaging yourself and begin to get along better with others. When you recognize your leadership style, you will have a chance to adjust it to align with the kind of people you lead and the corporate culture.

a) Who are you?

You can use this question for your life as a whole for general knowledge and clarity and then zoom in to answer it in the context of your workplace. This question will empower you to succeed well beyond your first-timer position. The more you know yourself, and most importantly, the better you can articulate it, the more you feel confident. This will position you to own your first-timer place, which we will discuss in the next chapter.

Here are some questions to consider answering, for your personal life, but in particular in your first-time leadership position:

- From where did I come?
- Who am I?
- Why am I here?
- What am I supposed to do here and now?
- Where am I going?

b) From where did I come?

Let me give you some pointers as you answer these questions for your current first-timer position. For this particular question, go back and review your work history. It reconnects you with your past. Don't be humble! Review your strengths, performances, and achievements. Going back down memory lane may boost your confidence, knowing that you have come a long way.

When we are overwhelmed with new responsibilities and feel inadequate, we forget that we felt the same thing in the past and overcame a lot. We forget how resilient we are when we are under pressure. Reacquaint yourself with your past. Pause and think about your past successes before you took this position.

c) Who am I?

For this question, forget what others may think. Ask yourself what makes you unique to qualify and take this leadership position.

In one statement, describe to an imaginary person in 60 seconds who you are. Do you feel the person is convinced of who you truly are? If you're not sure, take note and make it one of your growth development areas, which we will cover in the last chapter.

Remember, if you fail to eloquently narrate your own story, others will do it for you. When you allow others to define you, they will mostly misrepresent you. When that happens, it can create insecurity.

Now, stop and ask this question: Have you been in charge of defining yourself? Have you successfully communicated that to your people and stakeholders? If not, you have allowed others to describe who you are, and these narratives may not paint your true self. Control your narrative about who you believe you are and what that means to the leadership position you have taken.

Your success as a leader, now and in the future, is highly influenced by how much you know your true self but also by your ability to express it well. If you cannot articulate who you are and communicate it effectively, others won't know you. And, if they don't know you well, they struggle to follow you wholeheartedly.

Of course, I'm not encouraging you to engage in unproductive self-indulgence. Like everyone, you are unique. But as special as you are, so is everyone else, even those below your pay grade.

Now create a table with two columns. In the left column list your strengths and in the right your perceived weaknesses and limitations.

You need to tap into your strengths and leverage them. Be humble concerning your limitations and become vulnerable to grow in those areas or seek help. Request feedback from the people who know you best to uncover your blind spots. We'll cover feedback in Chapter 8.

Knowing yourself very well is so foundational that you should continue to grow in your self-knowledge. I like what Warren Bennis, one of the preeminent leadership gurus in the world, said: "Becoming a leader is synonymous with becoming yourself. It is precisely that simple, and it is also that difficult." Don't stop knowing yourself even long after you overcome the first-timer syndrome.

d) Why are you in this organization?

Simon Sinek, known for his insightful articulation of leadership concepts, wrote the influential book, *Start With Why*. We all should start our life, profession, business, or any other significant endeavor with a 'why.' Take knowing the why of your personal life as an assignment. For our purposes here, what is your 'why' for being in this organization? What brought you to this organization and to taking this leadership position?

Don't answer simply saying, "I'm here for the paycheck." Or "I saw a vacancy, and I applied, and here I am." These may be true on the surface but dig deeper. There may be a more powerful reason than these weak and temporal reasons. These won't help you increase your confidence to overcome the syndrome.

Ask yourself why questions until you get to the decisive reason that inspires you to get up in the morning, stay late, and go the extra mile. Then, ask a series of why questions till you uncover the reason you are inspired to take a risk and have decided to put more effort and hours into accepting your first-timer leadership position. It may go like this:

- **Question 1:** Why did I take this leadership position?
  Answer 1: Because of X.
- **Question 2:** Why does X matter to me?
  Answer 2: Because of Y.
- **Question 3:** Why is Y important?
  Answer 3: Because of Z.

Keep asking till you don't have any more questions left. Continue answering until you discover the very reason that motivated you to wake up early, work hard, and take your first-timer leadership position.

If your why is very strong, you will be convinced that the first-timer syndrome is worth experiencing. Most importantly, don't allow it to get in the way of living for your 'why.' This 'why' will persuade you to endure the pressure from leading others, some of whom may even be smarter than you. When you know that reason and connect it with your leadership role, there is no way that you will shrink from playing your role. You will be consciously willing to overcome whatever challenges you may face as you lead.

Okay, some of you may say, "Well, Assegid, I'm not like you. I'm here for the money or the perks and benefits." Even so, it is okay to start with these reasons that brought you this far. Going forward, discover and embrace more substantial 'why's'. The higher your cause - why you're there, the more motivated you'll be. The more you can capitalize on every opportunity you get to maximize your stay in the organization while also advancing its mission and serving its clients. And of course, you will be paid more, and will receive more perks and benefits. It is a win-win.

1.2. Know the main attributes of the organization

You might have had an orientation as a new employee or leader. Such formal orientations may give you some knowledge about your organization, but we are talking about digging deeper.

Do you know the organization very well? What makes you say that? From 1 to 10, 1 being "I don't know anything about the organization," and 10 being "I know how it was formed, the founders, its past, and am well aware of the ins and outs," how do you rate your knowledge?

If you scored less than 7, you should take this antidote seriously. Remember, what you don't know, you cannot manage. What you don't know hurts you, your team, and your organization. Below is the bare minimum of knowledge you should have about your organization:

1. History,
2. Mission and vision,
3. Strategies, and
4. Corporate culture and core values.

a) Know the short history of the organization.

Let's test your knowledge on this. If you're asked to show up in 5 minutes at the next orientation for new hires to share a brief history of the organization, could you do it? Try it, even if no one is giving you such an opportunity. Find a quiet place and imagine giving an orientation in that empty room. Your presentation should at least answer these questions:

1. When was it formed?
2. What caused it to come into existence?
3. Who were the founders?
4. What are the significant transformations/changes the organization has experienced?
5. What are its top success stories and challenges?

If you don't know the answers to some of these questions, figure out where to find them. Some of this info may not be available on the organization's website nor in the employee manual. You may need to conduct an informal interview with those who keep its oral history.

By all means, know your organization's history to serve it and its stakeholders with adequate knowledge. You should lead with your eyes open. You can better play a constructive role to enrich the organization's history and play your part toward making new history by building on what you have inherited. Not knowing the history, key players, stakeholders, and its significant transformations may hinder your effectiveness. You may also make some mistakes without even knowing it.

b) Know the mission and vision of the organization.

Do you know the 'why' of the organization? What is its mission? Stop reading and write down the mission. If you don't know it, check the website or your manual. If you cannot find a written mission statement, ask someone who knows it.

You have already discovered your own mission in life. Now you have learned the organization's mission. Is there any alignment between the two? I always tell people to make sure they share the mission of the organization they would like to work for. I also advise organizations to hire those whose personal mission aligns with the organization's or at least hire people who appreciate the organization's 'why.'

If there is a direct or indirect connection between your and the organization's mission, what are your and the team's contributions toward fulfilling that mission?

If there is no direct alignment between your and your organization's mission, what part of the organization do you love? Your personal cause may not necessarily need to align with your organization's. If you like who they serve or the products and services they produce, or some of the organization's values, it should be enough. By all means, you should consciously know the intersection points between you and the organization if you desire to own your place and demonstrate confidence, passion, and give your best.

The follow-up question is: What is the vision of the organization? In other words, where does the organization see itself in the future? Or where does the organization aspire to reach at the end of the day?

Write a single statement that expresses the vision of the organization. If you have to use just one symbol to describe the organization's vision, what would that symbol be? Why?

If you cannot articulate the vision of the organization, consult the website or organizational documents. If you cannot find a written vision statement, interview key players to develop a one-statement vision statement.

Do you share the organization's vision? How?

Then ask yourself: What would be the contributions of my team and my fair share in my current leadership role that would bring the organization to its highest level?

c) Know the strategies of the organization.

What strategies does the organization use to fulfill its mission and attain its vision? Strategies, simply, are major approaches an organization employs to achieve its grand goals. Below are some major strategies that many organizations use to fulfill their mandate:

- Products,
- Services,
- Sponsorships,
- Partnerships,

- Advocacies,
- Campaigns.

Of course, each department and/or team may use tactics under each strategy to fulfill their respective mandate. Knowing, at least, the major strategies of your organization facilitates your success as a first-timer. You may then identify the tactics your team should use that don't contradict the organization's overall strategy as you and your team meet your goals.

What are the major strategies of your organization? Which strategies are relevant to your team? What tactics are in place at your team level that will contribute toward the success of these strategies?

You may not find this info on the website nor in the company's publicly available documents. However, you can ask your supervisor to familiarize yourself with the strategic approaches of your organization. Then, you may need to recognize the tactics that are used by your team. If this is a new team and you have been given the flexibility to develop your own strategies and/or tactics, make sure they don't contradict the organization's overall approaches. They should align with the strategies of the organization.

d) Know the corporate culture of the organization.

Culture dictates how things are done in a given organization. Every organization has its own unique culture. When you study continually successful organizations, their culture is their competitive advantage.

They survive and even thrive in times of crisis, when others go down, because of their unique culture.

Experts in this area have identified four different types of corporate cultures for the following common types of organizations:

- **Hierarchical organizations** such as the military and many government agencies have a culture where decisions flow from top to bottom with limited flexibility.

- **For-profit organizations** such as Apple, Google, and many corporations create a flat culture that encourages individual team members to create and innovate.

- **Non-profits** like Red Cross, Feeding America, and World Vision create a culture that fosters cooperation and we-ness among team members.

- **Project-based organizations** such as NASA and many software companies and law firms don't have a particular uniform corporate culture. Each team and project may have its sub-culture that ends with the project.

Which among the above four cultures resembles your organization's culture? What made you say so?

Once you identify the type of corporate culture your organization has, describe the culture using 1 or 2 paragraphs. By doing so, you will see whether you have fully understood it. This will also show you whether you have some knowledge gaps. Answer these questions to help you figure out your corporate culture:

- How are things done around here?
- What are the norms, expectations, and taboos?
- What are some of the things that are encouraged, and what is discouraged?
- What does it take to succeed and fail in this organization?

If you can't answer these questions adequately, you're leading in this organization while blindfolded. You're also in for wild surprises and disappointments. You don't know where the:

- Treasures are hidden,
- Quicksand can be found, and
- Wild animals lurk.

If you are new and unable to figure out how things are done yet, begin learning the culture as soon as possible. The first place to start is by learning the corporate values of the organization. You may find these on the website or company documents. If not, strike up informal conversations with those who have been around for some time. Try also to put them in order of priority. Which three corporate values are dominant?

Once you are aware of the corporate culture, the next step is to make sure your team's subculture is aligned with the main culture. How your team does things should align with how things are done in the mainstream culture.

Play your part to avoid cultural misalignment, which may sabotage your overall success and future standing with the organization and its leaders. Cultural misalignments, wherever they may happen in an organization, negatively affect the greater good. They take away the potency of the mainstream corporate culture, and as a first-timer, you don't want to start your journey by contributing to cultural misalignment.

1.3. Know your job description very well

On top of knowing about the organization and its attributes, you should know your job description very well. You should:

- **Know the mission and goal of your team.** Why was your team formed? What is 'the main thing' of the team? Do you think the goal is achievable? Why? If you're not sure, don't worry about it right now. In Chapter 5, you will learn how to make your goals smart.

- **Know your job description.** Do you know your job description? Most of the time, you would know it before you even take the leadership position. In some cases, you may not know the full scope of your job description. There may also be responsibilities that aren't clearly defined. There could even be some unwritten expectations.

  If you don't have a formal job description, ask your supervisor. Write it down and share it with your supervisor to make sure you two are on the same page. Otherwise, even if you think you have fulfilled your job description by your own measure, unless your supervisor feels the same, you fail to meet her/his expectations. And this isn't good news. This isn't the way you would like to start your first-timer role.

- **Know the kind of leader you want to be.** That means, how would you like to be known and remembered? Having this clarity at this stage helps you decide how you would like to operate from the start. You become intentional about your words, behaviors, decisions, and actions. We will cover more on this in Chapter 9, where you will come up with your leadership philosophy that states what leadership means to you, your leadership style, what you expect from your team, what they should expect from you, how you prefer to communicate, and more. However, right now, at least, you should have an awareness of your leadership style. You should be conscious about whether it is helping or hindering you from succeeding

- **Know the areas you need to improve.** What areas in your leadership, such as your mindset, competencies, personality, or character, need improvements? You have to audit and have a sense of where you are right now. You cannot aim to go to the next level without marking where you start. We will further address this in the last chapter to identify areas where you would like to grow this year, your development goals, and your plan. For now, attempt to identify at least the major improvement areas that boost your confidence as a first-timer. Knowing this takes the pressure off. Sometimes we lose faith because we may have a subconscious feeling of inadequacy.

1.4. Know key stakeholders and their preferences

It may be impossible for you as a first-timer to know all stakeholders of your organization. And of course, you don't necessarily have to know them by name, other than those closely working with you. However, you should have a sense of who the key players are and their needs and priorities. Then focus on those who closely work with your team to meet their needs and work according to their preference and priorities.

- **Know the key decision-makers in the organization**. Which decision-maker(s) beyond your immediate supervisor has a particular interest in your team and what you do? What are their needs and expectations? Which stakeholders does your team interact with and communicate with regularly? Do you know their expectations of your team? How do you describe your supervisor? What are his/her goals, aspirations, needs, priorities, preferences, values, and pet peeves? If you don't know the answers to some of these questions, where do you get the answers?

Of course, you could directly ask them, but you won't get all the info you need unless you have already built a good relationship. Sharing intimate and personal preferences requires first building trust. If you think the latter isn't yet in place for some of these decision-makers, you should consider asking the people who closely worked with them in the past. You may also reach out to people who know them very well.

- **Know your team members.** Do you know who your team members are and their uniqueness? Why are they on the team? What is their 'why'? What are their professional goals, strengths, limitations, preferences, and aspirations? If you don't know the answers to these questions, how do you plan to learn? If you don't have good relationships and trust, they may not share what matters the most to them. Thus, first begin building relationships, be attentive, observe, and ask some thoughtful questions during a one-on-one to get to know them well. Again, what you don't know, you cannot manage.

- **Know end users.** Who are the end-users and other key beneficiaries that communicate with your team and benefit from its work? What are their needs? How do they prefer to share with you and the team? What are their concerns? Again, build relationships and trust, and make consistent efforts to know your end-users and beneficiaries. Next to your supervisor, end-users are those who, directly or indirectly, will evaluate your success. As a first-timer, these two groups should get your utmost attention. The more you know their needs and preferences, the more you and your team can serve them well.

ANTIDOTE 2

Own Your Place

"To be passive is to let others decide for you. To be aggressive is to decide for others. To be assertive is to decide for yourself. And to trust that there is enough, that you are enough."

Edith Eva Eger,

Holocaust survivor and psychologist

Knowing your place by having the necessary knowledge about yourself, the organization, your team, and other key stakeholders is a great start. However, knowledge is power if used properly and in a timely fashion. Knowledge that doesn't translate into results is useless in this case.

One of the first things you should do as a first-timer is position yourself as someone who 'owns the place' without appearing arrogant, cocky, or like a bully. The antidote in this chapter enables you to own your place. By the way, if you know your place well, owning your place becomes more effortless. Knowledge translates into wisdom and delivers when appropriately applied.

This antidote empowers you to leverage your knowledge and own your place. Owning your place means you talk, behave, and act as if you are in charge. As a first-timer, you need confidence more than ever. Once you become experienced in this, you may not need it as much in future leadership positions as you need it now.

The antidote in this chapter will equip you to feel confident and express that confidence without appearing arrogant or cocky. It is within your reach to lead assertively without bullying. It is possible to be confident while remaining humble.

Leading personal development expert, Jim Rohn, advised: "The challenge of leadership is to be strong, but not rude; be kind, but not weak; be bold, but not a bully; be thoughtful, but not lazy; be humble, but not timid; be proud, but not arrogant; have humor, but without folly." Leadership is about keeping the right balance. As a first-timer, you should focus on maintaining the delicate balance proposed by Rohn. I firmly believe that a leader can stand up for what she believes while at the same time make sure that she fulfills her new obligations without irritating others and damaging relationships. This chapter guides you to achieve just that.

Diagnostic questions
- In your current first-timer position or in the past, have you found yourself unprepared or ill-equipped?

- Have you heard a nagging voice inside that insists you aren't competent?
- Has your first-timer position been a celebratory moment, or has it ended up becoming a source of constant stress?
- Do you feel like you aren't capable enough for the current leadership position or the one you are aiming for?

If you have experienced one or more of the above signs, it's an indication that you may need the antidote offered in this chapter. Don't sweat it. These are common among first-timers. They go away when you increase your self-regard, and the antidote will secure your confidence.

As you may recall, in chapter 1 I said that increasing your self-awareness is the foundation for self-leadership. Self-awareness increases your self-regard as well. The more you know how unique you are, and what you bring to the table in your first-timer position, the higher your self-regard becomes and the more you will be able to own your place. This chapter offers some approaches in which you can leverage your knowledge from the previous chapter.

Owning your place means you have internal security that exudes on the outside for others to see and perceive. As a result, consciously or unconsciously, the people you lead and interact with accept you. They will be persuaded that you are someone who is up to the task of leading. On the other hand, unless you embrace yourself, no one else will. They know when you lack self-regard, which affects your ability to own your place of leadership.

Unfortunately, what we think and who we believe we are inside manifests outwardly, if only in subtle ways. Others around us perceive it. Our inner conversations and the narrations we run in our heads have power over us and communicate on our behalf to the outside world without seeking our conscious permission.

Of course, nobody consciously or intentionally thinks, behaves, or acts in ways that undercut themselves. Nonetheless, you may have counterproductive dominant thoughts at a subconscious level that leave clues for the rest of the world, telling them that you don't believe you deserve the promotion. You may also appear as if you aren't ready to lead, or not sure where you are taking the team.

The good news is that the previous antidote equipped you to bring subconscious thoughts into the conscious mind. You were awakened and recognized who you truly are, your uniqueness, strengths, and limitations. Now, you are aware of yourself, your surroundings, the people who interact with you, and most importantly, what unique proposition you bring to the table. This chapter will take it to the next level by empowering you to own your place by talking, behaving, deciding, and acting as if you are in charge of your new position of leadership. This antidote will equip you to:

- Demonstrate confidence,
- Become assertive, and
- Set expectations and the tone from the get-go.

Learning Objectives

The main goal of this antidote is to enable you to own your place by speaking, deciding, and acting confident. The following are the specific objectives:

- To increase self-regard by demonstrating confidence in your words, decisions, and actions from the get-go
- To overcome imposter syndrome
- To become assertive without appearing cocky or like a bully
- To set boundaries by setting parameters, deciding interactions, and setting expectations from the start.

2.1. Increase your self-regard

Though having confidence alone is not enough to succeed in any leadership role, its lack can hamper your success. It would help if you had the confidence within and were able to exude it on the outside to influence the people you lead. People can sense whether you are confident or not. Consciously or unconsciously, people around you pay attention to your words, decisions, and actions. Whether they know it or not, people measure you all the time, and how they size you up matters when you're a first-timer.

You can't own your place and be in charge without having confidence in yourself and your ability to lead in your first-timer leadership position. If you have come to know your place by now, you should have confidence. There is a massive difference between fake and real confidence.

One can look confident on the outside while experiencing deep insecurity within. You need the confidence that comes from knowing you are the right person with the right abilities to lead in your current role.

From 1 to 10, 1 being "I don't have self-regard or confidence at all," and 10 being "I act confidently, assertively, and set boundaries," where do you find yourself on this spectrum? If you scored less than 7, it's okay. You just need a high dose of this antidote, which helps you move on to the next confidence level.

Even if you rated yourself high, you might learn some additional insights and approaches in this chapter that will help you build on the confidence you already have. You can develop self-regard by:

- Exploiting your uniqueness in this leadership position
- Locating things that can position you to shine
- Taking some practical immediate and bold actions

a) Exploiting your uniqueness

Whether you're aware of it or not, some things prompted your promotion. Your manager may or may not articulate the unique attributes you have that led him/ her to promote you. If you figure out what makes you unique, this increases your inner confidence. When you're convinced within that you're worthy of the position, this will exude on the outside, generating confidence in the people you lead.

b) Locating what makes you shine

Even if you don't think you are unique or haven't figured it out yet, you can still carve a path for yourself to shine where you are. You simply need to be creative to come up with approaches that position you to be invaluable. Regardless of your inexperience or feelings of inadequacy, you can still boost your confidence if you find what makes you shine. You can use it as a competitive advantage that solidifies your confidence.

c) Taking immediate and bold practical actions

Once you identify your uniqueness and locate the things that can give you an edge to remain invaluable as a first-timer, you should come up with some practical, bold, and immediate actions right away. Don't waste time. You must assert and generate confidence before it's too late. The sooner you take bold actions that deliver results, the quicker you own your place. We will talk more about how to deliver results and increase productivity. For the latter, you have time. What I'm suggesting here are quick and bold immediate actions that allow you to own your place and generate confidence in you, your team, and other stakeholders.

2.2. Overcome imposter syndrome

If you succeed in the above three areas, you might be able to prevent imposter syndrome. Research shows that this syndrome is common among high performers like yourself. The difference is the degree. First-timers are more likely to experience imposter syndrome than are experienced leaders. Let me ask you:

- Have you heard of this syndrome?
- How do you understand it?
- Do you feel as if you are an imposter?
- What are some of the signs that let you know that you are experiencing imposter syndrome?

Experts agree that when one is infected with imposter syndrome, that person doubts him or herself and feels as if he/she is a fraud. It is believed that we all have this condition to some degree. Here are a couple of thoughts that signal that you've been afflicted:

- You question the judgment of the people who promoted you. Deep inside, you wonder whether you qualify or not, whether they made a mistake or not. You may constantly fear that they will come to their senses and regret promoting you.
- You attribute your promotion to pure luck. You may not gracefully say thank you when people congratulate you for your promotion. Instead, you might tell them that you just got lucky.
- You blame yourself for 'cheating' your superiors and tricking them into choosing you over others who were more qualified. You may also feel that you're a trickster who seems to be someone you're not.

The power of this syndrome is that you live, mostly in the background, in constant self-doubt. Unfortunately, this condition doesn't penalize you alone. It costs the people around you and the organization itself. You may even hurt your health. You may not give your best as you hide from being discovered. You won't aspire to go to the next level. You're already overwhelmed where you are. Imposter syndrome is a lose-lose for both you and your organization.

The good news is that you're now aware of the existence of this syndrome, and thus, you can do something about it. Start talking about it. Read more. Don't be ashamed of having this condition. The best in every field have been infected with imposter syndrome. The great Maya Angelo once confessed, **"I have written 11 books, but each time I think 'Uh-oh, they're going to find out now.'"**

From 1 to 5, 1 being "I feel like I'm a fraud and living each day afraid of being exposed," and 5 being "I accept myself, embrace my flaws, and am very comfortable about who and where I am," how do you rate yourself? If you scored less than 3, you need to develop some strategies to overcome imposter syndrome.

Take the following three steps to deal with imposter syndrome and reduce its impact on you as a first-timer leader:

- **Be aware of your inner conversation.** What are you telling yourself when you're alone? How do you react when people admire and appreciate you? Do you accept the praise and say thank you? Or do you deflect and claim that you're not as great as they think? Or do you accept it hesitantly, saying, "Yeah, I'm great on this but…"? Then do you disclose other areas where you're not doing that well? Such self-downgrading responses come because of the conversations you have within.

- **Disrupt the narrative.** When you catch yourself entertaining those self-damning and critical conversations within, stop and refuse to continue. You may simply rebuke the ego, saying, 'stop this.' It will obey you.

- **Begin to tell yourself how great you are.** Begin to appreciate what you are good at while working on those areas where you're not that good. Then, when others appreciate you, say thank you and absorb it without letting it into your head, leading you to pride or complacency.

Of course, the above quick antidotes are not enough. They only help you to lessen the impacts of the syndrome. You need to work on your confidence level by coming up with some long-term strategies. Think of this as one of the development areas when we get to the last chapter.

The following section will also further empower you to defeat the syndrome and stop it from sabotaging your smooth transition. The more you become assertive, the more you build your self-esteem and ultimately eliminate imposter syndrome eventually. Well-known Canadian-

American self-esteem psychologist Nathaniel Branden said: **"One of the ways you build self-esteem is by being self-assertive when it is not easy to do so. There are always times when self-assertiveness requires courage, no matter how high your self-esteem."**

2.3. Become assertive

Many shy away from taking leadership positions, especially emerging leaders, knowing that the responsibility requires making others accountable. You can't make others accountable unless you're assertive. Leading with assertion is hard for anybody, regardless of experience. However, it is more challenging when you're the new kid on the block. The most difficult scenario would be if you were promoted to supervise former colleagues (or even family members) who know you inside out and in which some team members are older or more experienced than you.

Your former peers and family members may struggle to separate you as the person they know from your responsibility as their leader. Some may even attempt to abuse the relationship to gain an advantage. That is why you should be assertive from the get-go and refuse to show favoritism.

You should also demonstrate assertiveness in your decision-making. Yes, it would be best if you were a participatory and consensus builder, irrespective of whom you're leading. But someone has to make decisions, sometimes alone, by taking sole responsibility. Being a junior leader shouldn't intimidate you or prevent you from making decisions assertively. You must understand that you were promoted partly because someone has to decide which direction a team will go. Assertive decision-making is especially necessary when there is no consensus among team members. Someone must take the lion's share of responsibility to set goals, agendas, and priorities for a given team. Of course, it's great to make decisions through consensus. But unfortunately that doesn't happen all the time. The leader must assert and, if necessary, make bold, risky, and unpopular decisions when required.

It's important to be assertive without being cocky or behaving like a bully. You should also be fair, thoughtful, and justify your decisions. If you explain how you make decisions, your team will likely understand why you must make bold decisions. We'll talk about coming up with your leadership philosophy and the importance of sharing it from the start so that your people can predict your actions and understand your position, even if they disagree with some of your decisions.

Below are some of the questions you should ask and answer to take your assertiveness to the next level:

- **Have you leveraged your top three strengths to continue leading assertively?** If you have taken a large enough dose of the first antidote, you should be clear about your top 3 strengths. The question here is: Have you leveraged these strengths to serve you in leading your team with assertiveness?

- **Have you been working on your top three limitations that may get in the way and challenge you from leading confidently?** We have already covered knowing yourself, including areas where you struggle as a first-timer leader. Here, the question is: What have you done to lessen the impacts of these weaknesses? What should you be doing to stop them from getting in the way and weakening your leadership?

- **Have you practiced assertiveness?** Have you made it a habit? What has worked and what hasn't? What changes should you make going forward? British writer, novelist, and screenwriter Warren Ellis said: **"The best gifts are never given, but claimed."** No matter how great your strengths, unless you use them, they won't help you become and remain an assertive and confident leader.

- **Have you audited to see whether your words, behaviors, decisions and/or actions are tentative?** 1 not assertive at all, 2 average, and 3 highly assertive. If you scored 1 or 2, what are your reasons for being tentative and less assertive? What are the root causes? Could it be the culture you grew up in or how you were brought up in your family? What else? How do you plan to address this issue?

- Take time and audit to see if your words, behaviors, decisions, and/or actions are tentative.

- Assess how these might have affected your confidence and the ability to lead.

- Quickly strategize to begin asserting on a small scale.
- You may need help from your mentor or those close to you as you practice being assertive within your inner circle before going out and trying it where the stakes are much higher.

Becoming assertive in your communication requires you to be intentional. You should take time to reflect and practice until it becomes second nature. Wherever you may be right now, don't become overwhelmed. Start somewhere. Assertiveness in leadership isn't only necessary as a first-timer; you need it as you climb the corporate ladder. You should demonstrate assertiveness by:

- Expressing yourself,
- Stating what you believe,
- Conveying your expectations,
- Uttering your agreements or disagreements without going overboard.

I'll leave this section on assertiveness with powerful advice from writer Doreen Virtue. She shared, **"Once you've got a major success with assertiveness, you learn that it's a much healthier path than being a doormat to the insensitive folks. You gain respect for yourself, have more time for your priorities, and develop authentic and healthier relationships."**

2.4. Set boundaries

Unless you set boundaries, people around you push you around. Once you allow this to happen, you become a pushover. And in turn, you lose your confidence and influence over your people. Below are some potential areas where you need to set boundaries:

- **Decisions.** How do you prefer to make decisions? Who will be involved? What are some exceptional situations where the usual way of making decisions may not work? The people around you should have a sense of how you make choices and the boundaries around decision-making.

- **Communications.** How do you prefer to communicate with your team, supervisor, and other key stakeholders? By now, you may already know the communication preferences of key stakeholders. Considering their preferences, what are some of the protocols you would like to establish and communicate back to them so that all parties are on the same page about how you and your team will communicate with these stakeholders? I'll give you some examples when we cover the communication strategies plan. At this point, make sure you are clear about how you would like to communicate with your team and other stakeholders.

- **Interactions.** What kind of subculture do you prefer to set up for your team that doesn't misalign with the mainstream culture of your organization?

Come up with some ground rules you would like to put in place to clearly state the acceptable and the unacceptable norms that form the subculture within your team. Once you are clear about your expectations, continue to reinforce them until they become part of the subculture of your team. Set an example, and appreciate those who abide by the cultural expectations while coaching and mentoring those who are struggling.

- **What else?** Depending on your objective conditions on the ground, you may consider additional boundaries. Be sure to write them down and communicate them with your team until they become part of the team's culture.

ANTIDOTE 3

Build Your Team

"Teamwork is the ability to work together toward a common vision. The ability to direct individual accomplishments toward organizational objectives. It is the fuel that allows common people to attain uncommon results."

Andrew Carnegie, Scottish-American
industrialist and philanthropist

The past two antidotes enabled you to know and own your new leadership place. These two are vital foundations for your success. Leadership begins with self. Knowing yourself, your team, other key stakeholders, your environment, and then owning your place play an important role in feeling, behaving, and acting confidently.

Chapter 1 explained the first antidote, which offered you a wealth of knowledge and showed you where to find it. Knowledge is power. Chapter 2 presented the second antidote, which empowered you to leverage your knowing to own your place. You learned how to think, talk, behave and act as if you're in charge without appearing arrogant, cocky, or like a bully.

Once you know your place and develop confidence based on your knowing, you own your place. These two antidotes focused on working on self, as effective and sustainable leadership begins with self. Though it is a good start, self-leadership isn't adequate by itself, especially for first-timers. As no one claps with one hand, you cannot deliver quickly without creating a team that functions like a well-oiled machine from the get-go.

The next important task at hand is to build your team. You've worked on your mindset and adjusted your attitude. You're feeling in charge. Now is the time to build your team. You can't succeed alone.

One person is too small, too insignificant, and too insufficient to achieve extraordinary results. You need a team that functions coherently. However, that doesn't happen unless you proactively invest your time and energy.

The good news is that antidote 3 will give you a head start to fast-track your team's growth to deliver quickly. This chapter will equip you to recognize how team dynamics work. It will also show you how to build a dynamic team that delivers results from the start. It is filled with guidelines to help you develop your team.

But, remember, you can't just build the team once and expect it to succeed and meet your expectations. You need to continually build your team throughout its lifespan, which we'll further cover in the last chapter. The key focus of this chapter is to give special attention to building your team right away to deliver quick results from the get-go.

Diagnostic questions

- Have you ever been assigned to lead a team in which everyone is pulling in a different direction?
- Have you had a team that was stuck, but you didn't know why? Even if you knew the cause, did you struggle to unstick it?
- Have you had a team that stagnated and failed to move forward with the speed you desired?

If you said yes to one or more of these questions, you aren't alone. These are common challenges faced by emerging leaders around the world. Maybe you inherited a team that got stuck in one of these scenarios. Don't panic. At the end of this chapter, you'll get the antidote. Your team will reach the performing stage and will stay there until it completes its mission or is reassigned to undertake another task.

Learning Objectives

The main objective of this chapter is to equip you to build a team that functions like a well-oiled machine from the get-go. The following are the specific objectives:

- To fully understand how a team functions and the stages they follow as they evolve until they begin to perform well.

- To position your team members to succeed by assigning them tasks in which they are interested and to lead the team with a team charter.
- To develop the team by bringing them together, coaching, and mentoring them, both one-on-one and collectively.

3.1. Understand team dynamics

Do you have a team? You may or may not have a team right now. If you have one, does every team member report to you? If some don't report to you directly, you should be strategic in influencing those who have their own bosses somewhere else.

Are your team members paid staff or volunteers? There is a vast difference in leading these two different types of teams and you should adjust your leadership style accordingly. You will have lots of leverage, and people tend to follow your instructions with ease when you're signing their paychecks. Of course, there are exceptions; there are some volunteers who are more committed than paid members.

It is a challenge to gain the full commitment of volunteers. You may not be able to do things as planned, as they may have other commitments elsewhere for which they are paid. They may not give your team the priority it deserves.

Though leading volunteers is a challenge most of the time, you can inspire, engage, and bring out their

A-Game. Put things in perspective and adjust your expectations. You should also immunize yourself against becoming frustrated when things aren't going your way or as planned.

If you don't yet have a team, make sure to be intentional about whom to bring in when the time comes to hire. Recruit those who share the mission and values of the organization and individuals who have the bare minimum skills, especially soft skills (people skills). Research conducted by Harvard University, the Carnegie Foundation, and Stanford Research Center revealed: **"85% of job success comes from having well-developed soft and people skills, and only 15% of job success comes from technical skills and knowledge (hard skills)."**

It takes longer to help people develop soft skills as compared to technical skills. Thus, hire those who already have them. Or recruit those who are willing to work on their people skills with a sense of urgency.

Once you have your team, you should have a Team Charter. If your team is a project team, craft a project charter instead. Discussing the latter is beyond the scope of this book, but you can easily Google some templates.

If your organization has a template, use the available one to draft the Team Charter together with your team. Let them own the charter by involving them from the start, as you all come up with the document that will govern the team. If your organization doesn't have a template, I have included a sample below. Feel free to customize it to fit your objective condition on the ground.

You may consider sharing the draft with your supervisor and requesting feedback.

- **Goal.** What is the goal of the team?
- **Scope.** What is the scope of your team?
- **Resources.** What resources are available to the team?
- **Progress Report.** How does the team prefer to communicate progress?
- **Outcomes.** What are the outcomes if the team succeeds or fails?
- **Stakeholders.** Who are the key players, such as the sponsors, decision makers, end users, and so on?
- **Signatures.** Let the whole team sign at the bottom of the charter. It's powerful when people see their names are enlisted and when they sign onto a charter. They take their responsibilities seriously and own the charter as theirs, not yours or the organization's.

3.2. Recognize team formation stages

Once you understand team dynamics, you should understand the five stages of team development. The Bruce Tuckman team formation model is one of the most recognized around the world. The model contains five major stages of team formation lifecycle:

- Forming,
- Storming,
- Norming,

- Performing, and
- Adjourning.

Team members come together during forming. The team then sets its goal, divides responsibilities among team members, and crafts a plan. When the rubber meets the road as the team implements its plan, it begins to experience conflicts. Storming is the most challenging stage, where team members may disagree, even fight over who does what, on priorities, methods, and resources. Norming happens once the team agrees to disagree and normalize its differences. At norming, things are relatively quiet compared to the previous stage. However, the team doesn't deliver well. Performing is the most productive stage, where the team performs and delivers. The team may remain at this stage until it is adjourned or assigned to take on another project.

Where is your team right now in the team formation stages? What led you to reach this conclusion? What should you be doing to take the team to the next stage?

Below are some pointers about what you should be doing to move your team to the next stage:

- **Forming.** Your job is to make sure that the team has a clear goal and everyone knows their assignments. You should also predetermine priorities, schedules, resources, methods, and approaches. If this is a project team, come up with a project charter. Include the essential elements of the project, and let the sponsors sign and authorize you as the project manager. You should also come up with a plan crafted by key stakeholders. If you succeed at this stage, you may not have a brutal and protracted storming stage.

- **Storming.** Always remember that this is a normal stage of team formation. Unlike what many leaders think, there is nothing wrong with you or your team simply because you're experiencing conflicts. Don't give up. Don't panic when you experience storming. Understand the sources, resolve the conflicts, and move the team to the next stage as quickly as possible. By the way, this is the stage that will test your leadership. As a first-timer, it can make or break it.

- **Norming.** Following storming, a team may not immediately be on the same page and deliver. The intensity of the storming determines how quickly the team can get unstuck. Your role at this stage is to help the team regroup, reenergize, and renew its commitment to fulfilling its individual and collective obligations. Remove obstacles, find common ground, and negotiate to take the team to the next stage.

- **Performing.** This is the stage where the team begins to deliver meaningful results. Your role is to create an environment that allows the team to perform and sustain that atmosphere until the group meets its goal and adjourns or is given another assignment. Otherwise, it may revert back to norming, or even storming.

If your team has to cease existing after performing and meeting its goal or completing a project, make sure to document lessons learned. Then, officially close the project and thank members and other stakeholders. Help the team that will take over the project from your team to make a smooth transition.

Sometimes, you'll continue to lead the same team but with the addition of new team members during the team's life. In such cases, an established team may start all over again from the forming stage and re-enter the dreaded storming stage. Don't get frustrated. Explain to the team what is happening. Help the group pass through the remaining stages to return to the performing stage.

By understanding the lifecycle above, you will develop awareness about where your team is at any given time. By recognizing your role during each stage, you will be able to play your part actively before your team finds itself stuck on a stage that doesn't allow it to deliver. You will also know how to take your team to the performing stage to fulfill its mandate and meet its goals.

Now that you have read these tips, let me ask you: What must you do to succeed at the stage your team is at right now and to take it to the next stage?

If you have led teams before and are aware of these five stages, which stage has been the most challenging for you? Why? How do you plan to overcome this challenge in your current and future teams?

3.3. Position your team members right

Now that you understand how teams develop and where your team stands on the team formation lifecycle, the most important task in building your team and overcoming first-timer syndrome is to place each member in a position where they function well. Let's assume that your team is formed and they are waiting for you to assign them tasks. How do you divide tasks among your team members? Do you assign or allow them to choose?

If you have never tried it before, I encourage you to be flexible in assigning tasks. People own the tasks they choose. On the other hand, I understand that you may not always want team members to choose. Some of the reasons could be:

• Certain tasks require qualifications/credentials
• Some 'unpleasant or boring' tasks may not be chosen
• Two or more team members may fight over certain tasks

Though you must deal with it if one or more of the above scenarios occurs, I encourage you to consider positioning your team members as per their preferences. Set each team member to succeed from the get-go by placing them where they have a competitive advantage. People over-deliver when they work on tasks they are passionate about. They give their best and deliver quality work.

Here are some practical tips:

- Together with your team, break down the project(s) into subprojects, and identify tasks to accomplish each subproject.
- Describe each task adequately.
- Assign who will do which task.
- Set a deadline for each.

To break down your project, you can use a graph like an organizational chart. At the top tier will be the project. Break down the project and put subprojects on the second tiers. Then break down each subproject to come up with tasks and even subtasks.

I also encourage you to maximize your real estate. On top of the project's name, subprojects, and tasks, you may include in each box, for instance, the number of people assigned, days to finish, and budget allocated for the project/subproject/task. This graphic representation gives added clarity to key stakeholders. For the bottom tier, you may consider writing the name of the team member who is assigned to accomplish that particular task or subtask.

Let's assume that your team is assigned to develop software for one of your organization's clients. You write the name of the software (or project) on the top box. Your subprojects could be:

- Requirement Analysis,
- Design,
- Coding,
- Testing,

- Releasing/Implementing, and
- Evaluation.

You then break down each subproject into major tasks. Some of these tasks might also be broken down into subtasks, if necessary, until one task is assigned to one person.

The graph clearly shows who is working with whom and on what. It also reveals whom to contact if needed. To further expand on this, you might also create an additional table that lists all tasks in the first column, description of the tasks in the second column, who is assigned in the third, deadline in the fourth, and remarks in the last column.

Post these two deliverables where key stakeholders can see them, both physically and/or virtually. Finally, don't forget to create versions. You may need to revise this document throughout the project's lifecycle. Creating versions avoids confusion and facilitates working based on the latest version.

3.4. Develop your team

At this point, your team might be ready and up to the task of translating your plan into a reality. Or it may need some work to execute the plan. Or it may not be ready at all. While leveraging your team's strengths to quickly deliver, which in turn boosts your confidence, identify the top areas where the team is weak. Then, strategize on how to develop your team to position it to undertake its mandate effectively from the start. Ask these questions:

- Should I send all or some team members to improve their competencies?
- Should I arrange in-house training on some of the skills that need to be developed?
- Should I hire a consultant or coach to assist me?

If the team is in good shape and doesn't need quick development, how do you continue building the team to prevent complacency and poor performance in the future?

Onetime development is not enough. You should keep building your team continually, which we'll cover in detail in the last chapter. Of course, your team could be ready in terms of its capacity to do its job without needing development. What might be lacking could be the ability to work like a well-oiled machine. This calls for a quick onsite or off-site team-building exercise to facilitate coordination so the team will march forward as one cohesive unit. Be creative to identify workable strategies to build your team.

You could also have a one-on-one with each team member. Decide the frequency. Should it be once per week or month? It could be every day, depending on the nature of your work. The goal is to make sure that you connect with each member regularly to acknowledge what they are doing well and appreciate their efforts.

You also need the one-on-one to recognize challenges and devise how you can support them to overcome these challenges. Please take this opportunity to build rapport with each member. Use it to demonstrate that you care about them. Let them know that you're their partner and are by their side in both the ups and downs they may experience. I have known supervisors who used this one-on-one to terrorize, belittle, and torture team members they don't like. Please don't do that.

You should have clear goals for each one-on-one meeting. Be thoughtful and take your time to be intentional with each individual. Of course, you should customize each session, too. You should also plan ahead of time and anticipate the unexpected.

Come up with a quick development plan to coach your team both collectively and individually. You have to invest in your team to get ROI in the form of productivity. Coaching primarily focuses on performance. Use coaching opportunities to speed up the individual and collective execution capacity of your team.

Identify which team members are performing well and coach them to go to the next level. Recognize those who are struggling and vulnerable, and support them to step up and meet/exceed your expectations. Depending on their specific needs, you may have to coach them yourself or else arrange coaching in-house or even from outside if necessary.

Consider also mentoring team members who may need work on their attitude/mindset and personality. The truth is, one bad apple can rot the rest. You need to identify attitude, soft skills, and character issues quickly and address them. Mentor and assist such team members in demonstrating the mindset and behaviors that align with the culture you are building.

ANTIDOTE 4

Communicate Effectively

"Effective communication is the number one tool to succeed in any endeavor. Effective communication determines whether people vote for you, write you a check, invest in what you do, buy your services and products."

Les Brown, American author
and motivational speaker

Knowing and owning your place and building your team set you up for success. Nonetheless, nothing will work unless you communicate effectively with key stakeholders. You won't benefit from knowing and owning your place without communicating confidently and articulately. And you can't build your team successfully without communicating effectively. Without effective communication, you are unlikely to overcome the first-timer syndrome.

Having a great team in place is a good start. But for the team to work together effectively and continue to perform well, you must have effective communication strategies. The antidote in this chapter will prepare you to connect with the people with whom you who work closely and to communicate with key stakeholders with whom you interact frequently.

By the way, lack of communication is not the problem. Interestingly, we communicate more than we think we do. I read an MIT survey that said scientists and engineers spend more of their time talking and writing than actually performing their technical work in the lab and workroom. Almost 70 percent of their time is spent talking, while around 10 percent is spent on actual technical work, and the rest on writing.

That means that 90 percent of their time is spent communicating verbally and in writing. Think about this: If professionals in *technical* fields spend most of their time communicating, imagine how much time professionals in other professions spend.

Of course, we are not talking about mere communication. We are talking about connecting with the people with whom you are working closely and with stakeholders with whom you interact frequently. Effective communication goes beyond simply talking and writing. It takes intentional and serious effort to connect. No wonder bestselling author and speaker on leadership, John C. Maxwell, said, **"Everybody communicates, few connect."**

Diagnostic questions

- Have you been communicating as a first-timer but feeling that you're not connecting deeply?
- Since you have taken your first-time position, have you experienced communication breakdowns, misunderstandings, and miscommunications?
- Are you struggling in certain aspects of your communication? Are these getting in the way of succeeding as a first-timer?

If you answered yes to one or more of the above questions, you have connection issues in your communications. This is a red flag for any leader, but especially for a first-timer. This begs you to give communication your immediate attention and priority. This chapter offers some quick fixes to remove those communication barriers that may be derailing your success as a first-timer.

Bad things follow when there is ineffective communication. The damage that can occur because of ineffective workplace communication may not be equivalent to a communication breakdown between a pilot and air traffic controller or between a lighthouse and a ship's captain, but it has undeniable implications that cannot be ignored. So, rather than cleaning up the mess that follows ineffective communication, it is better to be proactive and address it immediately. The antidote in this chapter is designed to help you do just that.

Learning Objectives

The main objective of this chapter is to empower you to communicate effectively as you put your first foot forward, leading your team to meet its goals successfully. Below are the specific objectives:

- To understand the communication choices of key stakeholders and align your communication to match theirs.
- To craft a strategic communication plan that guides your communication.
- To improve verbal and non-verbal communication and to listen attentively.

4.1. Understand stakeholders' preferences

Effective communication should begin by understanding the preferences of key stakeholders. You don't want to bombard your stakeholders with all kinds of information and communication methods. Instead, you should ask their preference in terms of content and delivery.

Some may prefer detailed communication while others specific data, such as the financial report. Some may not be interested in hearing about the progress you're making and whether there are challenges you're facing. They may simply be concerned about whether you will meet your deadline. Others may just want to know whether your project is meeting their expectations.

Once you know stakeholders' preferences when it comes to content, you should find out the method(s) they prefer you use to communicate with them. Some may prefer to communicate by email only, others by phone, in-person or through video conferencing, or a mix of all of these. Create an online or manual tracking system that includes the following:

- **Stakeholder**
- **Preference** (Report on Finance? Time? Milestones?)
- **Frequency** (Weekly? Monthly? Quarterly?)
- **Method** (In-person? Email? Phone? Paper?)
- **Remarks**. In this column, make notes concerning each stakeholder. If the preference of a given stakeholder changes, make note. If you are having some challenges with a particular stakeholder, make a note.

By the way, the above data is a good input for your communication strategies, which we will be covering next. However, the most important things to realize at this point in our conversation are:

- Your top communication preference may not align with some stakeholders.
- All stakeholders may not have the same preference.
- Not all stakeholders are interested in the same content and messages.

These realities beg that you align your communication style, approach, and methods with each stakeholder as per their preferences.

4.2. Craft a strategic communications plan

Successful teams have formal or informal communication strategies. They have a blueprint to follow for foreseeable and unforeseeable occasions. As a result, they don't experience miscommunication or communication breakdown. For each stakeholder and event, they know how to communicate, who will be communicating, and which method and tone to use.

If you don't have one, create one for your current team. Then, come up with a one or two-pager. The key is to clarify how you will communicate:

- Regularly among yourselves and other stakeholders.
- Progress.
- Announcements.
- During crisis.

You should also decide who will take the lead under each condition.

Having communication strategies in place enables you to be intentional and proactive in your communications. Consider the template below as a good start. Next, create a table using the elements below as columns.

- Communication type (for regular communication, communicating progress, press releases, during a crisis, etc.)
- Stakeholder (internal, ally, customer, press, rival, adversary, etc.)

- Strategy (formal communication, informal communication, socializing, mediation, and so on)
- Approach and frequency (in-person, virtual, chat, text, email; immediately, weekly, monthly, quarterly, etc.)
- Remarks

You may subtract or add new columns to meet your needs and the objective condition on the ground. Finally, draft the plan together with your team, solicit feedback from your immediate supervisor, and then share it with key stakeholders so you're all on the same page. Of course, it should be a live document that you can revisit occasionally to ensure it is up to date and up to the task of guiding your internal and external communications.

Don't forget, your communication will be tested not in times of order and quiet but during a crisis when all hell is breaking loose. We have seen how some national, organizational, and community leaders failed to communicate effectively during the COVID-19 crisis. True leadership is tested during a crisis.

Unfortunately, a crisis isn't the time to prepare. You must prepare well ahead of the curve. If you do, when a crisis hits, not only will you and your team know how to survive but you will thrive in the aftermath. This applies to both small and large-scale crises: at the team, organizational, and national levels. Get ready!

Of course, your communication strategies should be neither complicated nor formal. They should be simple, clear, and handy. The goal is to have a blueprint that everybody understands and follows.

For your purposes as a first-timer, you may not even need detailed formal communication strategies at all. You can simply have informal communication strategies for a couple of areas that guide your communication efforts. Some organizations, however, because of the nature of their work and the accompanying risks, craft detailed communication strategies in which everything is spelled out. Without offering much flexibility, the strategies are accompanied by detailed instructions, timeframes, accountabilities, and more.

Of course, you should regularly monitor your communication progress. Having a plan isn't enough. You should monitor and evaluate your progress and make changes as you go.

4.3. Develop all-around communication

As we have discussed, communication is necessary to connect at the end of the day. Connecting, however, takes the development of all-around and versatile communication. Therefore, multidimensional communication is a must to connect in 21ˢᵗ century work and marketplaces.

You might have already known your communication needs from Chapter 1. But in case you haven't had a chance to increase your awareness about your communication competencies yet, the key question at this stage is: What are some of the immediate communication areas you would like to improve right away to develop all-around communication?

Let me break it down a little for you. Below are some of the specific areas of communication you may need to work on:

- Interacting with people from diverse cultures, backgrounds, and religions;
- Active listening;
- Presentation skills;
- Leading team meetings;
- Providing constructive and tough feedback;
- Delivering bad news;
- Communicating via email;
- Conversations over the phone;
- Writing articles and blogs on the intranet to communicate your ideas;
- Communicating upward to influence your superiors;
- High-stakes communications, such as negotiating with critical stakeholders.

You can't work on all of these at once and effectively. You need to prioritize. You should come up with a plan to achieve these top priorities. If you're struggling to prioritize, we will cover in the next chapter how to prioritize. To overcome the first-timer syndrome, choose 1 – 3 major areas you need to work on right away, and then choose the next 1 – 3 areas to work on once you succeed on the first three. The priority should be on those communication areas that may sabotage your first-timer role the most.

We will further discuss communication skills down the road, such as delivering bad news, providing feedback, and conversing with superiors. Thus, you may not want to make them your priorities right now. Nonetheless, once you have more insight, tools, and approaches, you may want to work on them afterward. I will leave that decision to you.

4.4. Improve non-verbal communication & listening

One area many leaders, especially first-timers, neglect is non-verbal communication. This is a huge mistake. According to Albert Mehrabian, author of *Silent Messages*, likeability comes from 55% non-verbal communication (body language), 38% tone of voice, and only 7% verbal (spoken word). Can you imagine how much you're losing if you focus only on verbal communication, using email and other technologies without backing them up with visuals and your voice?

Below are some of the competencies you may need to improve your non-verbal communication:

1. Gestures;
2. Body language;
3. Eye contact;
4. Pause;
5. Facial expressions;

6. Presence;
7. Energy level.

Once you have identified your top non-verbal communication areas, work on them intentionally, and evaluate your progress. Join organizations like Toastmasters to get platforms where you can practice and receive feedback. You can also practice some of these in your private space by standing in front of your mirror and using informal opportunities as you communicate with friends and relatives during meetings, lunches, and dinners, without telling them you're practicing on them, of course!

Don't make the same mistake some emerging leaders make. They think that communication is a one-way street. As a result, they neglect listening. According to award-winning author Mark Shepard, **"By definition, communication means two-way communication. Insecure individuals don't like it. Bosses don't like it, but leaders and innovators do like it."**

Stop reading, and assess your listening ability. Are you a constant talker without the appetite to listen or are you an attentive and active listener? To improve your connection and to overcome the first-timer syndrome quickly, take your listening to the next level by coming up with some strategies.

To guide you in this journey of taking your listening to the next level, let me share with you the three levels of listening based on the listening model suggested by the authors of *Co-Active Coaching*:

- **Level 1** listening focuses on listening for self. The listener is preoccupied with understanding how what the other person is saying affects him/her and what to say next.
- **Level 2** listening requires attentively listening to understand what the other person has to say. The focus at this level is on the other person.
- **Level 3** listening requires going beyond what the other person is saying. It involves listening at a deeper level, including non-verbal and with emotions.

Recognize at what level you and your team members are listening.

It's imperative to understand that all of these levels are important, depending on the circumstance in which we find ourselves. For instance, if you're visiting your mechanic, you should listen at level 1 to fully understand everything he tells you about your car. Listen for you! And for your vehicle, of course.

On the other hand, if your team member or a stakeholder is sharing with you his/her happy moment or a concern or pain, you should focus on him/her and adopt empathetic listening. Listen for him/her!

When you find yourself conversing with someone on an issue that matters for both of you, you should adopt level 3 listening. This is especially important during conflict and when tensions are high. Level 3 listening entails paying attention to the emotions involved and the non-verbal cues as well. I like what management consultant, educator and author Peter Drucker said, **"The most important thing in communication is hearing what isn't said."**

Take a moment here to answer these questions:
1. At what level am I listening most of the time?
2. How can I take my listening to the next level?
3. If I'm at level 1, how can I take it to level 2?
4. If I'm at level 2, what should I be doing to take it to level 3?

I remember working on my listening, starting at level 1 and moving to level 2, and then to level 3. One method I used, which I copied from leadership guru John C. Maxwell, was when I went out to meet people, I would write on the top right corner of my notebook the capital letter 'L', to remind me to listen. I remember the struggle I had to grow from level 1 to level 2.

When working on level 3 listening, I remember paying attention to my own and to other's emotions and non-verbal body language. I still work on this last stage of listening, but I've come a long way.

When I listen to people now, I don't just assume that they are telling me everything, especially if we don't know each other and the issue is sensitive. Instead, I attempt to 'hear' at a deeper level, to understand if they have concerns or doubts. Sometimes, I get lucky and figure out what is happening in the other person's mind and am able to respond right there. When that happens, I can see right away when I connect with the person. Sometimes, I miss it but get it later. But be careful about this practice. You may end up not listening deeply at level 2 while trying to listen at level 3.

These days, I also attempt to help other people listen to me by communicating well beyond my words. I engage with my emotions, body language, voice, energy, etc. I also try my best to remove communication barriers between my listeners and me by being mindful and fully present. Are these efforts easy? Not at all. But they are worth the effort.

ANTIDOTE 5

Deliver Results

"The secret of getting ahead is getting started. The secret of getting started is breaking your complex overwhelming tasks into small manageable tasks, and starting on the first one."

Mark Twin, American writer,
publisher, and entrepreneur

By now, you might already know and even own your place. You might have already begun building your team speedily. You might also already be working on your communication. These all deserve your efforts if and only if you deliver quick results. Leadership, at the end of the day, is about delivering results.

Even though a leader must take care of the people and build processes and systems, her success is measured based on whether she has taken the team from point A to point B. The measuring stick is whether she has something to show; whether the team has met its goal or not. In the short term, stakeholders (shareholders) may be okay if a first-timer leader spends time doing the background work we have covered in the previous four chapters. After a while, though, they will expect tangible results.

If they haven't told you yet, the people who promoted you expect you to deliver. The question is how many weeks or months they will be willing to give you before they start to question whether or not you are the right person for the position. That is why you must make delivering results your top priority. Yes, there may be a gazillion things you need to do in the first couple of weeks and months until you can 'stand on your two feet.' But these efforts must lead to some form of results.

Once you work on yourself, your team and come up with the right communication strategies, this is the time to set goals, manage your time and energy effectively, and increase your productivity. The antidote in this chapter enables you to create goals and break them into manageable objectives and tasks. It equips you with prioritizing, scheduling, and protecting your priorities to deliver quick results. The latter elevates your inner confidence, as well as your team's confidence, and that of your supervisor's, leading you to easily overcome first-timer syndrome.

Diagnostic questions

- Do you have a team that isn't functioning like a well-oiled machine to deliver results?
- Though there are many activities and movements, are you lagging in meeting your goals?

- Do you have a great team that gets along but one that hasn't yet met stakeholder's expectations?
- Are you equipped and feeling confident personally, but are not sure whether your team is up to the task?

If you said yes to one of these questions, you need this antidote. First, you need to tap into your people's individual and corporate potential to deliver quick results. When that happens, your confidence and that of all parties is boosted. As a result, you will rid yourself of first-timer syndrome.

Learning Objectives

The main objective of this chapter is to deliver results sooner by setting your goals, managing your time and energy, and increasing your productivity. Below are the specific objectives:

- To write clear goals, identify the corresponding objectives, and tasks,
- To manage your time and energy effectively through prioritizing, scheduling, and executing successfully,
- To sustain your productivity by monitoring progress, conducting productive team meetings, and delegating correctly.

5.1. Set clear goals

If 1 is for setting goals while 3 is for translating goals into results, which resonates the most with you? Are you someone who is very good at planning? Or are you a person of action? Or maybe you keep the balance, and you are at 2?

Nothing is wrong with inclining toward 1 or 3. Both have their advantages. Based on our personality and leadership position, we may lean toward one of the extremes. However, the best place for first-timers is the middle, balancing the two by embracing both planning and executing.

The best way to keep the balance and deliver quick results is to have a clear goal. Have you used the globally recognized SMART approach invented by George Doran, Arthur Miller, and James Cunningham? If yes, did you like it? Did you get results? What were the challenges?

If you haven't used this approach before, SMART stands for:

- **Specific.** The goal is so clear that anybody, including people who don't have any expertise in what you do, should understand it.
- **Measurable.** The goal is quantifiable, allowing you to measure your progress.
- **Achievable.** You have the passion, know-how, and resources to attain the goal.
- **Relevant.** The goal contributes toward meeting the mission of the organization and the department within which your team is functioning.
- **Timely.** The goal has a specific deadline.

Use the SMART approach right now to create your personal and team goal. If you already have a goal, use the approach and make your existing goals smarter.

By the way, if your team doesn't have clear goals, this is an excellent opportunity to create them with your team. Arrange a brainstorming session to craft SMART goals. Of course, I understand that you might have been given the goal, and you may not have any flexibility to create or modify your team's goal. If you find that you don't have much leeway in creating your team's goal, my advice is to influence upward. Get your boss's buy-in to involve you in the process of setting future goals.

If you are given the freedom to develop new, or at least refine, existing goals, you may consider involving your team. Here is one way on how to do collective goal setting:

- Create a table on a whiteboard or flipchart.
- Give 5 stickers to each team member.
- Let them stick under each alphabet of the SMART approach what they think may make the goal smart.
- Collect the stickers and consolidate, since some of the ideas may be similar.
- Consider further discussion once everyone expresses their thoughts in writing.
- If you cannot reach a consensus, you may even use voting to decide the final goal.

There are some benefits in involving your team (if necessary, even some key stakeholders) to collectively craft the team's goals. Team members:

- Make the goal doable, as each member contributes to making it better. Two (and sometimes more than two) heads are better than one.
- Own the goal and feel like it is their goal rather than yours or the organization's.
- Give their best for the success of the goal.

Once you develop the team's goal(s), break them down into sub-goals and finally into manageable tasks.

Recall our earlier discussion about breaking your project into subprojects and then into tasks? Do the same to break down your goals:

- The top box is your goal.
- The 2ⁿᵈ tier represents objectives.
- The 3ʳᵈ tier contains tasks necessary to achieve each objective.

Consider doing this right now. First, break down your goal into objectives and tasks. Then, as needed, break down some of the tasks into sub-tasks.

Question: When should you stop breaking down a task any further? I stop breaking down a task if I know one person can take care of it. I then give that person the autonomy to decide whether or not to break down their task. Post the chart where your people can see and review it (in person and/or virtually).

5.2. Manage your time and energy effectively

Once you have clarity about your goals, the next stage is assigning team members and setting a deadline for each task. The latter requires managing time and energy wisely. As the father of modern management, Peter Drucker, said: "Time is the scarcest of all resources."

We can't replenish time. Once it is gone, it is gone forever. As the saying goes, time and tide wait for no one. And time doesn't care who is who. It keeps ticking, whether you're rich or poor, young or old, black or white, male or female. C.S. Lewis, British philosopher, writer, and theologian, said: **"The future is something which everyone reaches at the rate of 60 minutes an hour, whatever he does, whoever he is."**

Let me ask you, have you been treating your and your team's time with the care it deserves? If you answered yes, what helped you to succeed? If you said no, what prevented you from doing so? Have you used technologies, models, and approaches to manage your time effectively? What are the results?

I'm hoping you're not like many leaders who manage time efficiently rather than effectively. These leaders try to save one minute here, another there, and so on. They enter the rat race. Even if they save time here and there, they may not be effective. They may burn themselves and their team out. They may even hurt their health and relationships by neglecting to do the right things first.

Effective time management requires:
- Having clarity (clear purpose/goal),
- Strategizing/Planning,
- Prioritizing,
- Putting the top priorities on the schedule first,
- Executing your plan, and
- Protecting your priorities.

In the next section, I'll show you how to prioritize. For now, I'll give you some pointers on how to implement the other responsibilities. When it comes to strategizing, we've already talked about how to come up with strategies to fulfill the mandate (mission) of your team. But, make sure your team's strategies and tactics align with the organization's overall strategy. Once you have your strategy in place (you might have already been given these from your boss), come up with some tactics and plan for short (quarterly) and medium terms (1 – 3 years).

Your plan doesn't have to be an elaborate one. You can have a one-pager table. List major milestones in the first column. Describe each milestone in the second column. Assign people and resources to each milestone in the third column and the deadline in the fourth column. You may add an additional column to include notes about each milestone. Once you have the draft plan, the bulk of the work is breaking the short-term plan into monthly and weekly increments and then prioritizing weekly.

Once you have clarity about your top priorities (which we will cover next), schedule them. Then, without delay, begin implementing. Don't forget to protect your top priorities by saying no to lesser priorities. One of the great executioners, Steve Jobs, shared: "I'm as proud of many of the things we haven't done as the things we have done. Innovation is saying no to a thousand things." Frequently revisit your plan and priorities to make changes based on what is happening on the ground.

5.3. Prioritize

Prioritizing is essential for a variety of reasons. For instance, when you prioritize, you will:

- Gain further clarity. Some parts of your initial plan may not be feasible. In prioritizing, you might see that and refine the plan to make it attainable.
- Allocate your scarce resources to top priorities. You won't have unlimited resources to allocate indiscriminately, and thus, prioritizing assists you in deciding which tasks deserve your limited resources.
- Assign your top priorities to your top performers. Prioritizing helps you position your best team members to handle the most critical tasks.

Don't be like many leaders who invest their scarce resources indiscriminately on all projects, people, and tasks. One tool that is very well known around the world, which can assist you in prioritizing, is the 80/20 rule. If you stop and evaluate, you'll find that only 20% of projects, people, and tasks deliver 80% of the results.

I normally identify my 20% projects/tasks that deliver 80% of the results and then allocate 80% of my resources, including my time, on that 20% of projects/ tasks. With the remaining 20% of my resources, I can achieve at least 10% results if I invest in the remaining 80% of the projects and tasks that only deliver 20%. Using this simple principle to prioritize, I can increase my odds of delivering 90% or more results.

Of course, strategizing, planning, prioritizing, and scheduling aren't enough. Be sure to monitor your and your team's progress. Also conduct periodic evaluations to make changes if necessary.

Once you develop the habit of strategizing, planning, prioritizing, scheduling, executing, and protecting, you don't need to make any further effort. It becomes second nature. Let me give you the scientific data behind how long it takes you to develop a habit.

It has been believed for a very long time that it takes 21 days to develop a habit. However, the University of London recently suggested 66 days. If you take a rough average of the two, you may need at least a month to develop a habit. To learn more about how habits are formed and how to change unproductive habits and form new empowering ones, read *The Power of Habit* by Charles Duhigg, and James Clear's *Atomic Habits*.

Of course, on top of managing your time, you should also consider managing your energy. What is the use of saving time if you don't have enough energy to use it effectively? The good thing about energy management is that, unlike time, your energy is infinite. Therefore, you can generate as much energy as you know how to. Below are some of the things I do to generate and maintain my energy:

- Eat right. Eat and drink anything that will boost your energy while avoiding anything that drains your energy.
- Meditate and be mindful daily.
- Sleep well.
- Maintain work-life balance.
- Take rest and rejuvenate periodically.

I encourage you to measure where each team member is in terms of their time and energy management. Support those who need help the most to plan, strategize, prioritize, schedule, and protect their time. It is not enough if you are the only one with this competency and habit. You need each team member to excel in this area in order for the team to deliver results and continue to perform excellently.

5.4. Create and sustain your productivity

The above tasks will create productivity. Maintain your productivity by tracking your progress, conducting effective team meetings, and delegating. Coming up with goals and executing them to achieve results is a good beginning. However, sustaining the results is a challenge. These are important questions you should answer:

- How do you track progress?
- What does it take to set up and conduct effective meetings?
- How can you use delegation to enhance productivity?

a) Tracking progress

Consistent productivity is achievable if you are intentional. That journey should begin by setting performance goals for each team member and designing a monitoring mechanism to track progress. In Chapter 7, we will talk more about performance improvements. Here, we are talking about making quick and small consistent improvements to deliver immediate results that increase your and your team's morale. This will, in turn, overcome first-timer syndrome.

One stumbling block for many leaders, especially first-timers, is that they focus on activities rather than on results. Performance monitoring should be based on outputs instead of mere activities. Rather than measuring how many products one has produced or how many clients someone contacted, it should be based on the quality of the products and the clients' satisfaction. Focus on outputs rather than activities to track progress. Come up with some quantifiable matrix that measures results.

Of course, the monitoring should be periodic. You shouldn't wait till the end of the project or quarter. Monitor and make changes as frequently as possible.

b) Productivity tracking team meetings

Whenever I ask attendees who is looking forward to the next team meeting, very few hands go up. Since many team meetings are unproductive, people resent attending them. Of course, some suggest ditching meetings altogether.

You don't throw out the baby with the bathwater! Team meetings are necessary. In some projects, they are mandatory and included in the contract. Treat each of your meetings as a mini-project. Tap into project management principles to make your meetings so productive that people cannot wait to attend. Below are some measures you can take to improve your team meetings:

- Define the goal(s) for each meeting. If everything fails, what is that one thing this meeting must achieve?
- Identify the agenda and share it ahead of time with all participants. Because of their personality preference, some of your people may need time to think, process, and research before they communicate. If you invite them without a heads up, they may sit there without offering valuable input.
- Assign responsibilities to as many team members as possible to create ownership. Of course, some tasks require expertise, but be creative to come up with ideas to engage everyone. Create ownership by giving your people opportunities to participate in preparing and running these meetings. When you can do that, they will consider team meetings as

119

theirs, not just yours, and in turn will do their best to make them successful.

- At the start of each meeting, state the goal, time allocated for each agenda item, and the ground rules.

Depending on the stakes of the meeting, you may also wish to engage in discussions with some of the influential team members beforehand. John C. Maxwell once remarked that the meetings before the actual meeting are equally important. You rarely make important and tough decisions with the limited time you have during a single meeting. You may need to brainstorm and gather feedback ahead of time, at least from the key players. When you gather for the final meeting, it will be quicker and smoother if you have done your homework ahead of time.

c) Delegating to improve productivity

Delegation is one of the essential tools you should use with your team for various purposes. In Chapter 7, I'll deepen your understanding and offer you more tips on what, who, and how to delegate. But for now, let's focus on how you can become productive and deliver quick results by delegating effectively.

The goal of delegation in this chapter is productivity and how delegation can help you delegate fewer priority tasks so you are free to focus on those that bring greater productivity. Chapter 7's focus will be on how to use it to engage your people and accelerate their growth.

As a leader, you should know which tasks only you can do and which to delegate to others. You shouldn't handle everything that comes across your desk. Some tasks can be done by someone who is:

- More qualified,
- Experienced, and
- Paid less than you.

Excel in maximizing your scarce resources, time, and energy by delegating tasks to your team members, volunteers, and even your superiors. You focus on those tasks that can deliver quick results. Effective delegation saves time that you can spend on things that increase your faith in yourself and your team and vice versa.

One model I have been using and recommending to audiences in my workshops and also to my coachees is the 4Ds, invented by David Allen in his book, *Getting Things Done*. Let me walk you through how to use this tool to manage your time effectively.

- **D1**- Disregard (if it is an email, delete it). If the project/task doesn't add value, disregard it.
- **D2**- Delay (archive it). If the project/task isn't something to disregard, delay it.
- **D3**- Delegate (forward it). If the project/task isn't something that you can delay, delegate it.
- **D4**- Do it (reply). If you cannot disregard, delay, or delegate it, just do it!

Of course, the focus here is Delegate. Whenever a project/task/opportunity/request/email comes my way, I quickly run the 4Ds, and pick the right D. Don't always choose the last D right away. There are unworthy projects/ tasks that don't deserve to take up your precious time. To become productive and quickly overcome the first-timer syndrome, you need to know how to delegate to save time and use it to increase your productivity.

ANTIDOTE 6

Make Timely Decisions

"Time plays a role in almost every decision. And some decisions define your attitude about time."

John Cale, Welsh songwriter,
musician, and producer

As we covered in the previous chapter, leadership at the end of the day is about delivering results to meet the expectations of key stakeholders. You can't remain relevant in your leadership if you fail to deliver. And as a first-timer, delivering quickly is one of the antidotes to overcoming first-timer syndrome.

Yes, you had been delivering results in the past. That was why you were promoted to your new leadership position. However, in your new position, the stakes are higher. The organization and those who entrusted this position to you expect you to produce something fast so they can confirm that they made the right choice to put you in that leadership position.

The previous antidote equipped you to set SMART goals, manage your time and energy effectively, and create and sustain your productivity. The antidote was designed to make you a man or woman of results. It offered you models and tools that allowed you to deliver tangible results within a reasonably short time.

Nonetheless, you can't deliver quickly if you aren't equipped to make timely decisions. Maybe you've never made any high stakes decisions as a star employee. Maybe you were merely executing your boss's decisions. Now, you are on that hot seat. You'll be the one making decisions to roll the ball forward.

You are just starting to feel the pressure of leadership. It doesn't get easier when it comes to decision-making. So buckle up. To be honest, the more you advance in your leadership, the more problems and challenges you will face. You will be called upon to make decisions, sometimes without having adequate time or enough data.

You may already know this. But in case you don't, let me break this news to you. You have been promoted to make decisions. The whole team can't always sit down and make decisions every time. While you may pursue consensus decision-making by involving your people when time allows, there will be some decisions that you'll have to make alone.

Undoubtedly, you were making decisions in your past positions. Otherwise you wouldn't be here. Decision-making isn't new to you, except that as a first-timer, the stakes are higher, and stakeholders are watching.

The challenge of first-timers is that they may not yet feel comfortable making quick and tough decisions in their new position. You may want to avoid rocking the boat too soon or inadvertently stepping on someone's toes. These are legitimate concerns, especially for emerging leaders, and those who find themselves in a new leadership position.

Of course, depending on whether you're a CEO at the top of the food chain, a manager in the middle, or a new supervisor, the decisions you have to make will be different in scope and consequences. But regardless of where you are in the hierarchy, you have to make timely decisions, and this requires developing the right attitude, having some tools, and developing specific competencies.

As a first-timer, your true leadership will be tested when you are confronted with choices, and you have to make quick decisions without having enough info or time. Ready or not, you must make decisions from the get-go. The question, of course, is whether you are making timely decisions. Anybody can make the right decision if they have comprehensive data and enough time to think, reflect, gather info and consult others. The good news is that this chapter will treat you of indecisiveness. Wherever you may be on the decision-making continuum, it will take you to the next level.

This chapter reiterates the place of decision-making in leadership, especially for first-timers. It reminds you that you don't have a real problem unless you are forced to make a decision. The antidote in this chapter will help you differentiate between situations, realities, and problems. It then provides you insights and a tool many leaders worldwide use to solve problems promptly. It also equips you to develop a process as you make decisions, preparing you to make sound and timely ones as you pass through tough times.

Diagnostic questions

- Have you been infected with decision paralysis?
- Have you found yourself failing to make immediate decisions or making poor decisions in a hurry because you didn't have much data to consult or time to reflect?
- Have you struggled to make decisions because they are too close to make a call?

If you answered yes to one of the above questions, you need this antidote. This chapter is for you.

Learning Objectives

The main goal of this chapter is to equip you to make decisions timely. Below are the specific objectives:

- To understand the importance of being decisive,
- To recognize the significance of solving problems promptly,
- To develop a process that enables you to make right and tough decisions on time.

6.1. Understand the importance of decisiveness

Have you worked for an indecisive leader? What was it like? What were the consequences? Do you want to work for such a leader again?

I'm assuming that you don't want to work for an indecisive leader. I do also believe that you don't aspire to become such a leader. If so, that is great.

Likewise, I'm sure you have worked with decisive leaders in the past. Who do you consider the most decisive leader? This could be a national leader from the past, a leader at home or where you work now, or even one in sports or in the marketplace. What do you think enabled this person to be so decisive? In other words, what are some of the qualities of this leader that made him/her decisive?

Which of these qualities do you already have? Which ones do you need to develop? For those qualities you don't have right now, how do you plan to work on them?

To encourage you to develop the qualities of a decisive leader, let me share some of the benefits of becoming such a leader. Decisive leaders:

- Earn the respect of stakeholders, even those who may disagree with their decisions
- Can solve problems promptly and before they cause havoc
- Decrease the possibility of demoralization due to indecision
- Resolve disagreements fast before they become toxic conflicts

- Accelerate the forward advancement of their team by removing barriers

6.2. Learn how to solve problems promptly

One of the benefits of being decisive is that you are able to promptly address problems before they cause major issues. Problem-solving and decision-making feed into one another. Problems necessitate decisions. Decisions solve problems. To solve problems quickly, you should have these three in place:

- Differentiate problems from issues and realities,
- Have a framework that guides your problem-solving,
- Engage as many stakeholders as possible in seeking sustainable solutions.

Issue vs. Reality vs. Problem

Many leaders spend countless hours and invest their scarce resources in situations that aren't inherently problematic. If you dig a little bit, a given situation could end up being one of these:

1. An issue,
2. A reality, or
3. A problem.

Some situations are just issues. If you wait, they go away without you having to make any decision. There are also realities on which your decision will have no effect.

You don't have control. But if a situation isn't an issue or a reality, it is a problem that necessitates a decision.

A situation is just an issue if it doesn't stop you from pursuing your goal. If you still can do your job with a bit of inconvenience, it could just be an issue that dissipates with time. Be patient. Don't waste scarce resources such as your finances, time, or energy.

Let's be practical. Right now, without overthinking it, list all the situations you have, both personal and at work. Then answer the following two questions:

- Which of these situations is stopping you from pursuing your goals?
- Over which ones do you have influence and control?

If a given situation doesn't come between you and your team's goals, it's not a real problem. Unless you have some form of control and influence over a situation, you cannot fix it. It's out of your scope, and therefore is not your problem unless, of course, you want to make it yours. If it doesn't demand a decision, a situation isn't yet a problem.

Once you have clarity about the true nature of problems, you should have a framework or model that you use to facilitate making decisions and solving problems on time. Most problem-solving models available today share some of the following common stages. Of course, you can customize the framework below and continuously improve it to make sure it is serving you in solving problems promptly. It is a tool, a means, not the end itself.

a) **Defining.** Understand the problem before analyzing and trying to fix it. As I indicated earlier, make sure it isn't merely an issue or a reality. If you define it, you can analyze it. If you analyze it, you have a fair chance to resolve it.

b) **Analyzing.** Once you have properly defined the problem, the next step is analyzing it by gathering data, interviewing people familiar with it, and researching. You should employ critical thinking and use data gathering and analysis tools.

c) **Resolving.** Come up with alternative solutions that could solve the problem by using decision-making tools. Before you implement your top decision that could solve the problem, get approval, if necessary.

d) **Implementing.** Fix the problem using the top option.

e) **Evaluating.** Monitor to determine whether the solution you decided on has addressed the problem. If yes, problem solved. Celebrate your success. If no, redefine the problem to come up with an alternative option. If you had multiple alternatives during the Resolving stage, you don't need to start from Defining. Instead, simply choose the next option, implement it, and see if it fixes it. If not, continue to go through the options until you exhaust all the options you came up with.

Make sure your team learns from each problem so that if similar problems resurface, your team doesn't start the process of solving from scratch. Use your organization's internal learning platform or learning management system to archive problems that have been fixed so that your people will first visit this portal to search using keywords. They shouldn't start from scratch to troubleshoot and address problems that had already been tackled. Even if the new problem is a little different, they can learn from similar past problems to accelerate fixing the new ones.

If your organization doesn't have an intranet knowledge management platform or if creating one isn't feasible in the short-term, consider creating local files or a database, or use a hard copy record-keeping system within your team.

6.3. Three sources of power in decision-making

One of the qualities of decisive leaders is that they have a well-tested process that assists them in making tough decisions on time. On top of understanding the nature of problems and how to address them systematically, they have a preferred source(s). Hence, to overcome first-timer syndrome quickly and to go beyond decision paralysis, you should learn from experienced decision-makers.

Below are three major sources of decisions that you should consider as you make decisions. Leaders at all levels make decisions, whether they're conscious about it or not, by relying on these three sources:

1. **Insight.** Based on what you observe, hear, and read in the present.
2. **Intuition.** Gut feeling based on your past experience.
3. **Algorithm and supercomputers.** Based on well-designed algorithms, using the processing power of supercomputers.

Some decisions are made best when you have insight. However, sometimes, you may not have reliable data, or finding and gathering such data may take too much time. Unfortunately, you may not have such time. In such cases, you may be left with trusting your intuition, or your gut feeling. Of course, you may tap into both sources.

Realize that the more leaders advance in their leadership and therefore make tough and consequential decisions without enough data and time, the more they rely on their gut feeling. The founder and CEO of Amazon, Jeff Bezos, once said, **"I believe in the power of wandering. All of my best decisions in business and in life have been made with heart, intuition, guts, not analysis."** Of course, using one's gut feeling as a source of decision doesn't mean the leader wings it based on some unrecognized voice within. Only naive leaders heed such an inner voice. Experienced leaders have already trained themselves on how to listen to their intelligent self, which uses the vast database that has been built for years.

As a first-timer, you may not need to make many decisions based on your gut, at least for now. But, if you have to, make sure you also first consult the data available to you. Use your intuition but also gather as much data as possible to make accurate decisions.

You probably won't be making decisions based on algorithms. For your information, some organizations depend on algorithms and supercomputers to make tough decisions. The nature of their work requires them to over-depend on an automated system that makes predictable decisions. For example, one of the top hedge fund companies in the world, Bridgewater Associates, uses algorithms and high-processing machines to predict the market and make quick decisions involving millions and sometimes even billions of dollars.

Let me show you the difference between making decisions using gut feeling and insight. Gary Klein, who has done a great deal of research on decision-making, said: **"Intuition is the use of patterns you have already learned, whereas insight is the discovery of new patterns."** While intuition is about the past, insight is about the now. It is wise not to over-depend on past experience or what one sees now. What happened in the past shouldn't preoccupy us to the point of missing golden opportunities now and in the future.

We should keep the balance. If you're over-dependent on your gut feeling, you trust your past rather than your present and future. You may be unwilling to consider new info and perspectives. Thus, your decisions are always predictable and based on what has worked for you in the past. If you're over-dependent on insight, you're missing lots of historical perspectives and what has been already tested and has worked. You may be repeating the same mistakes again and again in your decisions.

Watch also whether you have some recognizable biases in your decision-making, identified by experts in the field. Ask these questions:

- When I make decisions, do I always look for inner confirmation?
- Do I place greater emphasis on recent happenings?
- Do I focus on what is dramatic?
- Do I turn over all stones?

Once you recognize your bias(es), make sure to challenge it/them. Let's say your bias is analysis paralysis, where you overturn all stones before you make a call. You should question this bias. One way to counter your bias is to find facts that counter it. For instance, you have this bias because you might have a strong believe that you must get 100% of the info to make the right decision. Here is one advice that counters your belief about how much data you should gather before you make a decision. Former Secretary of State and four-star General Colin Powell has a 40/70 rule, in which he says, **"Never make a decision with less than 40% of the information available, and don't gather more than 70% of the information available. Anything less than 40% and you're just guessing, anything more than 70% and you're delaying."** If you delay your decision to gather more data, you may end up overwhelmed and make wrong decisions because of information overload.

Even if you know your sources of decisions and you are a great decision-maker, you may not have the prerogative authority to make particular decisions as an emerging leader. Or you may be required to get approval before you implement your decision. In such cases, you should know how to sell your choices to superiors.

Unless you excel in getting buy-in from your supervisors, some of your quality decisions (solutions, requests, proposals, ideas, etc.) may not be approved and implemented. Whether you present your decision verbally or in writing, consider the following template I came up with after studying many frameworks over the years:

- **Executive summary**. What are the essential elements of your proposal, such as its goal, benefits, and proposed solutions? Include here if there are some crucial facts and figures in the document. The decision-makers may not read the whole proposal unless your executive summary grabs their attention.
- **Background and problem statement**. Why does this issue matter? What is the context? What is (are) the problem(s) that need(s) to be addressed? Ensure your description of the problem convinces the decision maker(s) that it is worthy of their scarce time, energy, and resources.
- **Goal and objectives**. What would be the end goal? What are the specific objectives?

- **Method and participation.** What problem-solving approach(es) have you used? Who was involved?
- **Solution and alternatives.** What did you decide? What are the top three alternative solutions in order of importance?
- **Benefits.** What are the advantages of your number one choice? Why is that your top choice? Who will be benefiting?
- **Drawbacks.** Are there any disadvantages to choosing your number one solution? Who will be impacted? What are some of the consequences?
- **Conclusion and call to action**. What are the key points and recommendations? Make your call to action specific and easy to execute.
- **References.** You may also want to include references and details. Indicate in the body of the proposal which index at the back of your report they should refer to for detailed data.

You may take this as a starting point to come up with your own. Continue to refine and tailor it whenever necessary and according to the target decision-maker(s).

6.4. Deciding amid conflicts & impasses

You may not always make decisions without challenges. Depending on the nature of your work, you may sometimes have to face conflicts and impasses where you cannot quickly make decisions and move on. As a result, things may not always go the way you want, and with the speed you desire.

You might already know: Conflict happens everywhere. It occurs in the boardroom, in the labs, on the streets, at home, everywhere. There is, however, one place you may not find conflict. Where is that, you may wonder? You guessed it - in the graveyard. That means facing conflict isn't a bad thing at all. It shows that your team is alive.

Since conflict is common and you cannot prevent it entirely, you should learn the nature of conflicts that surface frequently. You should also know how to turn conflicts into opportunities. Here are a couple of considerations when you make decisions amid conflicts:

- Recognize the primary sources of conflicts,
- Increase your awareness about how you handle conflicts,
- Move beyond an impasse and take care of relationships.

a) Major sources of conflicts in your team

From organization to organization, the sources of conflict vary. Still, the more you know the sources, the more you have a chance to address them quickly. These are some of the common sources of conflicts in today's work and marketplaces:

- **People-related.** Differences in personalities, choices, and preferences.
- **Technical issues.** Disagreements about which tool, method, or technique to use.

137

- **Implementation approaches.** Disputes over how a given project or change should be implemented.
- **External factors.** Conflicts with customers, regulatory bodies, allies, and/or competitors.

b) Increase your awareness

To increase your chance to come up with solutions and make quick decisions during conflicts, you need to increase your self-awareness. You should know your default approach when you face conflict. Unless you are aware of this, you will repeatedly and indiscriminately use the same style for all conflicts. Using the same style definitely won't work all the time.

In 1974, Kenneth W. Thomas and Ralph H. Kilmann introduced their Thomas–Kilmann Conflict Mode Instrument, which identified five conflict modes: Competing, Compromising, Collaborating, Avoiding, and Accommodating. Note that in normal circumstances, you may use all these styles. In a meeting, for instance, you may use many of these at once. However, when you first enter a conflict, you may zoom in and overuse one style over the others, which is unproductive.

I encourage you to learn more about the TKI (Thomas Killman Instrument). Take also the free version assessment online to know your most preferred and least preferred conflict modes. Then, if possible, take the paid version to get a more comprehensive report that provides you with some strategies for using your most preferred mode less often and your least preferred mode more often.

c) Go beyond impasse and take care of relationships

As a leader, you must make decisions and resolve disputes no matter how hard they are or who is involved. Don't be tempted to think they will go away if you ignore them for a while because you're afraid of harming the relationships.

It's great if you resolve conflicts with consensus. However, that may not always be the case when you have to make tough decisions that will not make all parties involved happy. It's okay if you cannot please everyone. Nevertheless, your preoccupation should be preserving the relationships. If people see that you care, empathize, and respect them while you're addressing disputes, even if they're unhappy with how you decide to deal with the conflicts, they will at least not take it personally. As a result, the relationships may not be damaged.

Even if you develop the ability to resolve conflicts and turn them into opportunities, some conflicts may not be solved without negotiation. You have to take time and follow procedure. That means you cannot simply decide your way out all the time. You may need to sit down more than once to negotiate a win-win deal. Here are three scenarios you may find yourself in during any negotiation. You may be negotiating with:

- People close to you and at home
- Co-workers and stakeholders
- Competitors and rivals

Depending on the relationship, you should adjust your approach. Don't treat all negotiations the same way. Below are the three widely accepted choices you have, both in normal and in conflict circumstances:

1. **Win-Lose.** You are aiming to win. You may choose this scenario when you deal with competitors and rivals. Some cultures encourage winning by any means. They reward winners who go out and get as many deals as possible for themselves. This approach damages relationships. It's not sustainable. You can't always win and get away with it.

2. **Lose-Win**. You are less interested in winning. Most of us use this approach when dealing with loved ones at home and sometimes with close friends and colleagues. We choose relationships over wins. However, this scenario often doesn't work in work and marketplaces. Your team and organization expect you to win, even if you may not be personally interested in winning.

3. **Win-Win.** This is obviously the best scenario. It allows you to solve the conflict and address the impasse without losing the relationships. All parties win. It is the most sustainable approach. Improving your negotiation competencies to succeed in win-win deals empowers you beyond your time as an emerging leader. You need this competency even once you overcome the first-timer syndrome. Keep working on it.

ANTIDOTE 7

Engage Your People

"In motivating people, you've got to engage their
minds and their hearts. I motivate people, I hope,
by example - and perhaps by excitement, by having
productive ideas to make others feel involved."

Rupert Murdoch, Australian American
billionaire businessman and media tycoon.

Your ability to deliver quickly as a first-timer gives
you breathing space as you assert in your new
leadership position. It allows you to demonstrate
that you can deliver results. You're up to the task.

You now have the necessary insights you need to be
a decisive leader from the start. The previous antidote also
armed you with some models, processes, and approaches
that will enable you to take to the next level your ability to
make timely decisions.

Continue to practice what you have learned to
become more decisive than you were before. The more

you solve problems quickly and make decisions promptly, the more you position yourself to succeed as a leader. You also take your team to the next level by helping them solve the problems that hinder them from moving forward. You can easily remove barriers that come between your team and their goals through decisiveness.

However, in order to continue delivering consistently, you must engage your people. You can't maintain the team's momentum to achieve results unless they are 'all in' throughout the life of the team. This takes having the right mindset, developing certain competencies, and using effective tools.

Though true and lasting inspiration comes from within, great leaders can motivate even the walking dead. Sadly, since first-timers are self-motivated, many make the mistake of thinking that others are also self-motivated. They assume that a paycheck and some tangible benefits are enough reason for people to be motivated and engaged. They also use the same things that motivate them to give their best to draw out results from others.

At this point, you may have some team members who aren't as engaged as you had expected them to be. Realize that the overwhelming majority of people join an organization or team to have a meaningful impact. But, unfortunately, something might have happened that disengaged them. It could be the system or you as their boss or other team members.

Whatever caused some of your team members to demotivate or to be less committed, you need to find out what it is and remove it, if your desire is to engage your people and tap into their full potential. As a first-timer, you need the full engagement of everyone to overcome first-timer syndrome. You should draw out their A-game by consistently engaging them to the fullest.

The antidote in this chapter will enable you to understand the place of engagement. It equips you with the necessary insights and tools to continually motivate your people. You will also learn the power of being grateful and using proper appreciation that works. You will learn how to delegate effectively to engage your people and deliver consistently, which is critical to go beyond first-time leadership pitfalls.

Diagnostic questions

- Have you inherited a team that is dead, and you don't know how to revitalize it?
- Have you faced a team that doesn't engage, and you tried everything else, and still don't see engagement at the level you desire?
- Have you led a team that is in plateau state; a team that exists but doesn't look like it is alive?

If you answered yes to one or more of these questions, this antidote is for you. It equips you to engage your people, and that will, in turn, increase your level of confidence.

Learning Objectives

The main goal of this chapter is to empower you to engage your people through inspiration, proper appreciation, and effective delegation. Below are the specific objectives:

- To understand how people are motivated and create an environment that inspires and engages
- To tailor your appreciation and recognition to continually inspire your team
- To use effective delegation as one means of engaging your people

7.1. Engage your people by knowing their motivation

We all have things that we value the most; things that inspire us. However, what motivates one person may not motivate another. One's needs may not be the needs of another. We are different, even though we have so many things in common.

The first job of a leader is to demonstrate motivation. You can't give what you don't have. Unless they see that you are motivated and passionate about what you do, you don't have the authenticity and influence to expect motivation from your people. Second, a leader must find what motivates others. Remember, you are self-motivated, and that was why you were promoted. However, that doesn't mean those who seem unmotivated in your team can't be motivated. There are things that motivate them.

You should figure out what those things are. Third, once you understand their needs, engage and motivate them.

For centuries, leaders have attempted to inspire others to do great things. As a result, many theories have been developed to support leaders in motivating their people to accomplish extraordinary results. Even in the 21st Century, some of these theories can still provide insight.

For instance, Frederick Taylor's scientific management theory focused on efficiency. He suggested managers treat employees like parts in a production line to increase productivity. Unfortunately, those leaders who follow his advice micromanage their people. Rather than engaging their people, they opt for controlling, and do not have sustainable results.

Social psychologist Douglas McGregor created Theory X and Theory Y, which recognize two contrasting sets of assumptions that managers make about their people. Those who believe in Theory X describe employees as people who don't like work, are without drive, and are reluctant to accept responsibilities. Those who believe in this theory assume that workers are there for a paycheck and need supervision.

Those who believe in Theory Y rightfully assume that people love their work, desire autonomy, find meaning in their work, and have a sense of pride in what they do. As a result, they are flexible, engaging, and supportive of their people. I encourage you to disregard Theory X. Go for Theory Y to motivate your people through engagement.

Of course, you should still be flexible. Part of being flexible is to believe that everyone doesn't have the same motivation. Don't use a blanket approach to treat everyone the same. The best approach to engage your people is to understand what motivates them individually.

The question then is how do you figure out what motivates each one of your team members? Some of your people may easily and comfortably tell you what motivates them. However, others may not be willing to do so right away. In this case, you may need to develop a rapport with them first or be vulnerable and share what motivates and engages you so that they will open up and share what motivates them.

You might also ask the people who work with them what engages them most. Understand what motivates them individually and give it to them. Listen to Dwight D. Eisenhower, who said, **"Leadership is the art of getting someone else to do something you want done because he wants to do it."** You cannot achieve this level of success without the ability to fully engage your people.

Think about a time when you were highly motivated and engaged as a team member? What did your manager do to motivate and engage you? Go the extra mile to motivate your people just like your former manager did. Conversely, think about those times where you were highly unmotivated. What happened? Understand this, and don't let it happen to your people.

7.2. Engage your people by meeting their needs

We all have needs throughout our lives. Abraham Maslow's Hierarchy of Needs is as follows:

1. **Physiological**: Food, water, air, etc.
2. **Safety:** Employment, security, health, and so on.
3. **Belonging**: Love, friendship, intimacy, and so on.
4. **Esteem**: Respect, appreciation, freedom, etc.
5. **Self-actualization:** Fulfillment, attaining full potential, mastery, and so on.

People aren't motivated by needs that are already met. To engage your people and motivate, find out which needs are unmet and find ways to meet their top needs within your prerogative authority. You may not have a great deal of flexibility for those team members who have the first two needs from Maslow's pyramid but you can create friendships and a sense of belonging in your team, which doesn't cost money or require approval from higher up. You can respect, appreciate, and recognize them when they do great work. You can also create an environment that challenges and allows them to tap into their potential and improve their craft.

More than any other single factor, your attitude toward your people plays a crucial role in motivating them. Are you appreciative of who they are and their work? You may feel appreciation within but unless you communicate it on the outside it doesn't matter.

Here are a couple of things you can do to demonstrate appreciation:

1. In your meetings and one-on-ones, make sure to express your appreciation to your people as a whole. Mention specific examples of why you're appreciative.

2. When you see something extraordinary, like someone staying behind to finish a task after work, don't wait until the next day. Instead, express your appreciation right away. At least say thank you for doing this in person, over the phone, via email, or whatever method is appropriate.

3. Appreciate individual efforts publicly. On top of appreciating your team's corporate engagement and performance collectively and in private one-on-one settings, you should also appreciate exemplary work in public to set an example. However, be very careful about public praise. It can backfire unless it is justifiable in the eyes of the other team members.

7.3. Engage your people by using proper recognition

The fourth need from Maslow's hierarchy of needs is recognition. There another theory that shows the power of recognition as well, which is Herzberg's two-factor theory. This theory underscores that employee satisfaction has two dimensions: Hygiene factors and Motivation factors.

Hygiene factors are extrinsic to the work, and are:
- Pay
- Work conditions
- Employee relationships
- Bad policies, procedures, and so on.

Motivation factors are intrinsic to the work, and are:
- Challenging work
- Autonomy
- Opportunities to grow
- Recognition

Hygiene factors do not motivate people, but satisfying these needs doesn't guarantee motivation. They only stop complaining.

It is crucial to address those hygiene factors for which you have control and authority. Nonetheless, your focus on engaging and motivating your team should be on those motivation factors that are intrinsic to the work itself. You may or may not have the flexibility to use the other motivating factors, but I'm sure you can use recognition as a gateway to motivate your people.

Have you been recognized in the past? I'm sure you have. Do you remember why? What made the recognition unforgettable? Come up with creative ways to recognize your people and tailor each recognition according to the preference of each member. This will make it unforgettable for them, just as it was for you.

7.4. Engage your people using effective delegation

We talked earlier about one aspect of delegation. We have seen how you can delegate less important tasks to others to increase your productivity and invest your scarce time on tasks that add value. Delegation is also very powerful to engage people. However, many leaders are afraid to delegate. Have you delegated in the past? If not, what scares you about delegating?

Many leaders hesitate to delegate because they:
- Feel others won't do the job the way they do it.
- Believe it takes them less time to do it themselves.
- Fear losing control.
- May not know how to delegate appropriately.

Of course, there are essential tasks you should never delegate:
- Aligning your people with the mission, vision, and values of the organization.
- Providing direction for your team.
- Recognizing team members for a job well done.
- Offering feedback on poor performance.
- Disciplining for misconduct.

If you're still unconvinced about the need to delegate, let me tell you the most important benefit of delegation: Engaging your people. Delegating some of your responsibilities shows your people that you:
- Believe in their abilities.

- Trust their judgments and decisions.
- Would like to see them grow.

These things engage your people exponentially. Once you're convinced and willing to delegate, get clarity about the purpose of your delegation. There are at least two purposes:

1. To save time, and
2. To provide growth opportunities.

If you are delegating to save time, what kind of tasks should you be delegating? The key parameter is whether these tasks occur frequently. If not, why delegate?! If it happens once in a blue moon, you'd better do it yourself. Otherwise, you may spend lots of time and resources to train someone without the benefit of saving time. You may actually spend more time than if you do it yourself.

If your goal is to give your people growth opportunities, time should not be the decisive factor. You may spend time and energy upfront with the hope that you will get your return on investment down the road. Right now, list all your tasks and decide which ones you would like to delegate. Then determine which ones to delegate and which ones to keep for yourself.

Remember, delegation isn't a one-time act. You should keep track of your delegations. Learn some lessons yourself to improve future delegations. You should also provide performance feedback to your delegatees to help them grow and become better next time.

To help you succeed in delegating, find a framework that works for you. There are some delegation models out there. Feel free to customize the model below, which I use and recommend to my audience and coachees. You may also wish to improvise, adding or subtracting elements to it. By all means, use the one that works best for you.

1. **Purpose.** Why the delegation? What are the reasons for this delegation, both individually and organizationally?

2. **Vision.** What would you like to see at the end of the delegation? Is the goal understandable to the delegatee? Can you show or demonstrate what the end outcome looks like?

3. **Scope.** What is the scope of the delegation? What is acceptable and what isn't acceptable? Where are the quicksand and wild animals?

4. **Success measures.** What are the indicators that determine success?

5. **Resources.** Whose help does the delegatee need? What are the material, financial, and other resources required?

6. **Progress.** How will the two of you communicate progress?

Ask questions and give the delegatee ample opportunities to ask questions before you hand over the assignment. Sometimes, they may quickly say "I got it" and go out and do something you didn't ask them to do. If they don't have any questions, that could be a sign that they didn't absorb everything. In such cases, it doesn't hurt to ask a couple of questions to make sure they understand what is expected of them.

By the way, you can use the same framework when something has been delegated to you by your boss or one of your peers or team members. Knowing these steps helps you to ask the right questions before you take the assignment.

To practice what you have learned from this chapter using the above model, delegate a task to one of your team members next week. Follow each step and practice. Remember, if you are just starting to delegate, you may not do it right the first couple of times. Continue to practice. Once you master it within your team, you should consider delegating to your peers, volunteers, and then to your superiors.

ANTIDOTE 8

Strive for Excellence

"The foundation of lasting self-confidence and
self-esteem is excellence, mastery of your work."

Brian Tracy, Canadian American
author and motivational speaker.

The previous antidote equipped you with
competencies that allowed you to engage your
people through motivation, appreciation, and
delegation to keep delivering outstanding results. These,
nonetheless, are not enough to completely overcome first-
timer syndrome. You should elevate the performance of
your people by increasing the excellence level of your
individual members and the whole team. That is why the
antidote in this chapter is vital. It will take your team's
productivity to the next level as you embrace excellence
to create and maintain a team that performs continually.

This antidote equips you to set individual and
collective performance goals and review them to ensure

they are achieved. It also empowers you to give performance feedback to your team. This chapter also prepares you ahead of time on how to deal with poor performers.

We humans are very much controlled, consciously or unconsciously, by what we value. Our attitudes, behaviors, decisions, and actions are dictated by the values we embrace. One of the most powerful values of extraordinary leaders is excellence. You can't become a successful leader by chance or by behaving, deciding, and acting casually. You need to have something that drives you consistently, like excellence, to build on your individual and collective achievements. Otherwise, you will soon end up complacent and remain mediocre. As a first-timer, you don't want that to happen to you.

True leaders value excellence and impart it to their team. It is one of their competitive advantages. That is why Peter F. Drucker noted, **"Leadership is not magnetic personality, that can just as well be a glib tongue. It is not 'making friends and influencing people,' that is flattery."** Instead, he emphasized, **"Leadership is lifting a person's vision to higher sights, the raising of a person's performance to a higher standard, the building of a personality beyond its normal limitations."** True leaders believe in excellence and stretch their people to bring their best by tapping into their unlimited potential.

Diagnostic questions
- Do you have a complacent team?
- Have you inherited a team that doesn't innovate and continually create?
- Have you found yourself unable to measure the performance of your people?
- Do you struggle with how to provide constructive and challenging feedback, especially to those performing poorly?

If you said yes to one or more of the questions above, you need the antidote in this chapter. It provides you insights, tools, and approaches that will help you become excellent and empower your people to excel, which in turn will alleviate the impacts of first-timer syndrome.

Learning Objectives

The main goal of this chapter is to encourage you to embrace excellence to continually improve your team's performance. Below are the specific objectives:
- To recognize the significant place of excellence in leading a constantly performing team,
- To set and manage performance goals, including for those who are performing poorly,
- To create an environment that encourages feedback giving and receiving, which contributes to excellence and continual performance improvement.

8.1. Recognize the place of excellence

When you hear the word excellence, what comes to mind? Do you know someone whom you consider a person of excellence? What are some of the qualities they have, which allowed them to be a person of excellence? Which of these qualities do you have, and which ones do you not have?

In the 21ˢᵗ Century, one can't influence using title and authority alone. One of the world-renowned thought leaders, Robin Sharma, pointed out, **"Leadership is less about the position you hold than the influence you have. It's about doing world-class work, playing at your peak, and leaving people better than you found them. It's about Leading Without a Title."** One way to earn the commitment of your people without exerting your title is to be excellent at what you do.

Here are a couple of truths about excellence. Excellence is:

- **A mix of having both the right mindset and some competency.** Excellence is more of an attitude than it is a skill. Unless you have the right attitude that honors excellence, you won't take the trouble to master your craft. For sure, mastering your craft requires some competency. However, you won't persist in improving those competencies in your field unless you are persuaded that the effort is worth the trouble.

- **Not complex.** Contrary to many who complicate excellence, it is simple, and when it is present, anyone can recognize it. One of the most influential Africa American educators, Booker T. Washington, said it very well: **"Excellence is to do a common thing in an uncommon way."** It takes someone becoming creative and innovative in small ways and daily to excel in what they do.

- **Accessible to anyone.** Everyone has the potential to excel if they are willing to prevail in what they do. Decorated military general Colin Powell demystified the notion that excellence is for a few extraordinary people. He declared, **"Excellence is not an exception; it is a prevailing attitude."**

- **Not a mystery.** You can recognize, develop, and measure excellence. It is quantifiable. Greek philosopher Aristotle said, **"We are what we repeatedly do. Excellence, then, is not an act, but a habit."** Excelling at anything doesn't come with one shot. You need to develop some essential habits to live up to your excellence value. Show me your dominant habits, and I can tell you your excellence level.

Excellence without the development of certain habits is hard, if not impossible. Here are a few quick considerations as you work to develop certain habits that empower you to excel in what you do:

- **Identify habits that lead to excellence.** Study the people you consider excellent and identify their top habits.

- **Develop the habits.** One day at a time, even if you don't feel like doing those things that lead you to excellence, do them. After a while, they become second nature. You don't need to think and make great effort once the habits are formed. The latest research by the University of London, which I mentioned earlier, suggested that it may take up to 66 days for a habit to stick.

- **Cull the sabotaging habits.** Study successful leaders and observe what they don't do. If you have habits that are not common among great leaders, it's time to get rid of them. They are getting in your way and preventing you from excelling. Starve these counterproductive habits, and they will die.

- **Persist.** To keep building good habits and get rid of bad ones, you need persistence.

Of course, developing the right performance habits is the start of a prolonged journey as you master your craft. You need more than 66 days to master anything. These days are required to form the habits. Performance researcher Anders Ericsson has done intensive research on how mastering your craft may take years. Using Ericsson's research results, Malcolm Gladwell, Canadian author and public speaker, popularized the 10,000-hour rule, that says achieving mastery of a field takes roughly 10,000 hours of practice. Wherever you are on this spectrum, continue to master your craft by putting daily hours toward improving your competencies.

8.2. Set and manage performance goals

Once you're convinced of the importance of excellence and what it takes to excel, it's time to start raising the bar on yourself and your team. Becoming exceptional individually and collectively requires becoming intentional, strategic, and systematic. You should:

- Have performance goals and a plan
- Execute the plan
- Measure your results
- Monitor and evaluate your progress and continually improve upon your creativity and innovation without seizing.

You may recall we talked about SMART goals. You should have SMART performance goals for the team and for each team member. Come up with goals that can be achieved, but at the same time are challenging enough to force you and the team to become creative and innovative.

Using these performance goals, you may come up with a plan, go out and execute it, and measure your results to see if the goals and outcomes are aligned, and whether you met your performance goals. Keep upgrading your performance goals as you meet the existing ones. Then, as you succeed, continue to aim higher. I like what basketball coach Rick Pitino said: **"Excellence is the unlimited ability to improve the quality of what you have to offer."**

Create a database to keep a record of the performance of your team. It will help you track your progress. You can also use it as an early warning system, as it shows you who is meeting the performance goals and who is struggling, so you can step in before things go south.

If you already have your own and the team's performance goals, take time to make them more measurable. If you don't yet have such quantifiable performance goals, take this as an assignment to develop your team's performance plan. Use some measurement parameters relevant to your field as you craft these goals. Don't forget to involve your team when you come up with the performance goals of the team and their individual performance goals.

Ownership is critical for people to play their A-game. Besides, it's easier to strike up feedback conversations based on their own performance target goals. If they fall short of meeting their own goals, ask them questions about what might have kept them from reaching those goals, what lessons they learned, and what they should do going forward.

Make it a culture for your team to talk about performance in group and one-on-one meetings. Decide the frequency with your team. Then, meet as planned to provide feedback, help your team, and make progress on the go. You might consider making performance reviews every quarter or less.

When you find yourself dissatisfied with your own and the team's performance, don't delay. You should regroup, evaluate, and make changes right away. Don't wait until the end of the year. Instead, track your progress on the fly. If necessary, make adjustments on the goals themselves and/or their implementation to take your performance to the next level.

8.3. Give performance feedback

Providing feedback is very important, but many leaders don't do it at all or do it badly. In both cases, they shouldn't be blamed. Providing feedback is hard, especially negative feedback. However, as a first-timer leader, if you haven't yet, you should begin to provide feedback to your people and your superiors. Of course, providing feedback to your bosses is beyond the scope of this book, but take note and make it one of your future growth goals, which we will cover in the last chapter. One of the qualities upper management looks for from junior leaders like yourself is your ability to offer constructive feedback to your peers and supervisors.

For now, let's focus on how you should give proper performance feedback to your team members. I'm sure you have given feedback before. How do you feel about your past ability to provide feedback? Do you think you did it properly? Did your feedback improve performance? If not, what was lacking? To help you assess your past feedback approaches and make adjustments, let me give you some tips.

Overall, in the workplace, we can divide feedbacks into three types:

1. **Instant feedback.** You give this feedback on the spot, whether privately or publicly. Such instant feedback can't wait or doesn't make sense if you do it later. For instance, if you can't hear someone over the phone or in a virtual environment, ask them to speak up. But don't give instant feedback that can wait. Performance feedback can wait at least until the next break.

2. **Performance-driven feedback.** You should make providing performance feedback a culture. People need to know where they stand in terms of their performance. You can use feedback once in a while to let your people know what is working that they should keep on doing and what areas need improvement.

3. **Growth-centered feedback.** You may decide to grow some of your team members to succeed you or someone else. You need to give them opportunities, such as delegation, to learn the ropes, and then give them periodic feedback to help them grow and become better.

Here, our focus is giving performance-driven feedback. The Center for Creative Leadership has a nice model called Situation-Behavior-Impact. Most feedback-giving models share these three steps. First, you state the situation you're concerned about, the behaviors you noticed, and the impacts of these behaviors. After that you can use this model as is or customize it to fit your objective conditions.

After trying several versions, I came up with the following steps based on how I have been giving feedback that has worked for me. I will bypass some of the steps when necessary. Try it, and feel free to modify it for your own use.

1. **Set the stage.** Choose your timing and place. Don't give performance feedback publicly. Find a private spot. Don't offer feedback if the person isn't in the right mood. If she just lost one of her family members, that is not the right time. If she is preparing to go on vacation, that is bad timing. But don't wait too long to give feedback. It should be given before they forget it.

2. **Be as specific as possible.** Don't beat around the bush. Go directly to the issue at hand. State the Situation and Behaviors. Let them know from the start why you're there. Give them specific examples of the performance behavior you noticed and the impact you're attempting to alleviate. It might go like this: "I'd like to talk to you about your report (Situation). You were supposed to submit it at the end of last week. Instead, you submitted it early this week (Behavior)." If you wait for the employee to respond, you don't need to ask any follow-up questions. They will tell you the very reason why

that happened. After listening carefully, explain the Impact of their behavior.

3. **Offer suggestions(s).** After explaining the impact, you may ask them first to suggest a fix to alleviate the impact. Then, if you're not satisfied or if you have a better solution than theirs, suggest it.

4. **Come up with a plan of action.** You can simply ask, "How do you plan to address this performance issue?" If they don't come up with a good plan or if you have a better one, propose it.

5. **Monitor and evaluate.** Set milestones to measure success and how the two of you will communicate progress.

Here are a couple of considerations as you give feedback:

- **Make it conversational.** Ask instead of tell. Listen instead of talk. Create the feeling that you two are one team and are there to address the common issue as partners. Put aside your boss's hat for a while.

- **Avoid being judgmental**. Don't come to premature conclusions.

- **Listen attentively.** You must understand the situation well by listening actively. Don't listen at level 1, listen at level 2 and 3.

- **Demonstrate care.** The person is more important than the situation that caused the performance issue. Regardless of how significant the impact has been, treat the person with respect and empathy. You can be tough on the issue but soft on the person.

- **Show flexibility.** Don't make up your mind too soon. Be open to being influenced on how to address the performance issue.
- **Be supportive.** Performance issues take time to resolve. Be patient and render support until the performance issue is resolved.

8.4. Address poor performance issues right away

You will rarely have a team that has all A-players. There are so many factors that may prevent you from having high performers. You may not have been given the authority to choose or hire your team members. They may have been assigned to you without your input. Whether you have team members who were poor performers before joining your team or team members who were performing great but then began lagging in meeting their own performance goals, it is up to you to turn the situation around. You should know how to address poor performance within your team. This is one of the prices you pay as a leader.

It is not pretty, but you have to do it. The more prepared and experienced you are in handling poor performers and troublemakers, the more you can address the issues without major impacts. And by the way, the quicker you overcome first-timer syndrome. If you wait or hesitate to address such problems because of a lack of assertiveness, you will pay the price down the road. Here are some ideas to be proactive and intentional:

- **Be vigilant and proactive.** Identify poor performers on your team before a problem surfaces and impacts other team members and the team as a whole.
- **Strategize and plan.** Craft some strategies and plan on how to help poor performers improve their performance.
- **Sit down with poor performers.** As quickly as possible, once you have done your homework, you need to meet and talk with each poor performer.
- **Schedule follow-up sessions.** Every week or every other week (whatever works for you), schedule a one-on-one session to review their performance and offer feedback.
- **Give support.** Offer your support.

Here are some steps you can take to address poor performance with individual team members:

- **Identify the root cause.** A poor performance could be just a lack of discipline and may require disciplinary measures. Or it could be due to a lack of knowledge and skills or a lack of the right attitude or soft skills. Mark Murphy, the author of Hiring for Attitude, reported that **"46% percent of new hires fail in the first 18 months, and 89 percent of them failed for attitudinal reasons. Only 11 percent failed due to a lack of hard skills."** Is the root cause behavioral, technical, and/or related to people skills?

- **Give feedback.** When you notice that one of your team members is performing poorly and lagging, identify the root cause and follow the feedback method suggested earlier.
- **Set expectations ahead of time.** If you don't see improvement, let them know the process you will be taking if they don't improve. For instance, you may give them one oral warning, another in writing, and finally, you may have to let them go. Before you decide to let them go, you might provide them with an opportunity for counseling, if it is available.

It's crucial to understand how the company policy works before you lay out the process concerning how to deal with chronic poor performers. You may need to work closely with Human Resources on this. Talk to other supervisors and also to your manager. But those who are performing poorly deserve to know the process you will be following. You shouldn't surprise them. Remember, even if you may not care about someone who is performing poorly, you don't want to set a bad example for other team members. You need to send the right signal of how you will treat them if they happen to fall from grace.

Using the above framework next week, provide performance feedback to one of your team members. Make sure to write it down first. Practice and anticipate pushback and/or resistance. Start it on a small scale. Give one piece of feedback at a time, and make sure your goal is not to criticize, belittle or judge the team member. The end goal of providing feedback must be to improve performance. Give 1 - 3 pieces of feedback on what is working and 1 - 3 on what may need some improvement. Provide one example of each.

ANTIDOTE 9

Articulate Your Leadership Philosophy

"The quality of a leader is reflected in the standards they set for themselves."

Ray Kroc, former CEO of McDonald.

You have learned from the previous chapter about the need to create and support a team that continually performs. You have also understood the significant place of excellence at the early stage of your leadership and how embracing excellence could help you overcome complacency and mediocrity from the get-go. As a first-timer, if you heed the advice of actor Robert Forster who said: **"If you deliver excellence right now, that gives you the best shot at the best future you've got coming,"** you can go beyond the syndrome to enjoy a bright future.

Leaders who don't challenge themselves end up second-rate. They fail to raise the bar for themselves and their teams. The most challenging but sustainable way of overcoming first-timer syndrome and staying relevant is to consistently improve your performance. You can self-improve without competing with others. This determination should begin while you're still an emerging leader.

However, striving for excellence individually and collectively to outperform needs to be complemented with a personality that allows you to continually influence. So far in this book, you have been working on your mindset, attitude, and competencies to succeed in your first-timer leadership position. This chapter is designed to help you define your personality. Whether you are conscious of it or not, whether you are deliberate or not, you are dictated by certain philosophies that influence your attitude, behaviors, decisions, and actions.

These philosophies define your leadership style(s). As a leader, not only should you be aware of these philosophies that are leading you behind the scene, but you should be in charge of deciding the right and most productive philosophies to substitute for those that are not productive. Chapter 9 is designed to equip you to understand what true leadership is and recognize the significance of your robust leadership philosophy to begin the journey to become a true leader. At the same time, you're still an emerging leader. Therefore, it will also assist you in crafting and communicating superbly.

The antidote in this chapter inspires you to become a true leader to overcome the syndrome and lay a solid foundation to become an impactful leader. There is no scarcity of leadership. There are leaders in many forms and shapes. What is lacking? The world desperately needs true leaders who have the personality and character to lead by example.

Let me ask you:

- Have you worked for and with a predictable leader? How did it feel? Would you like to work with that person again?
- Have you worked for or with a leader whom you couldn't figure out for months? How did it feel? How did it affect you?

Diagnostic questions

- Do you know your leadership style(s)? Have you been intentional in deciding which style is appropriate to which group of people?
- Have you discovered what matters the most in your leadership? Do you know your values? Have you articulated and communicated your core values? Have you shared, promoted, and defended your values?
- Do you have a leadership philosophy in writing? Have you articulated your leadership philosophy and clearly recognized what you expect from others and what they should expect from you?
- Have you shared your leadership philosophy with the people you work with?

If you said no to one of the above questions, you need the antidote in this chapter.

Learning Objectives

The main goal of this chapter is to help you articulate and communicate your leadership philosophy. Below are the specific objectives:

- To understand true leadership and how to become a leader,
- To recognize the significance of having a leadership philosophy that explains what you stand for and what matters the most to you,
- To learn how to craft and communicate your leadership philosophy.

9.1. Understanding the place of true leadership

Let's settle the basics before we talk about true leadership. You might be familiar with the debate about whether leaders are born or made. Though there may still be those who believe leaders are born, the overwhelming leadership practitioners and experts believe that leaders are made. For instance, one of the greatest football coaches, Vince Lombardi, acknowledged: **"Leaders aren't born, they are made. And they are made just like anything else, through hard work. And that's the price we'll have to pay to achieve that goal, or any goal."**

This is good news for first-timers like yourself. You'll be the one to determine your fate as a leader. Even if you may not have some inherent leadership qualities yet, you can develop them to become a great leader, which in turn shortens the impact of first-timer syndrome.

Now that we're on the same page about your leadership material, let's talk about true leadership. You might have worked with true leaders, and you may have some ideas about true leadership. Let me ask you:

- How do you define true leadership?
- What is the difference between ordinary leaders and true leaders?
- Who is your most admired true leader, either from history or now?
- What made her/him a true leader? In other words, what are this person's key characteristics?
- Which of these attributes do you already have? Which ones do you not yet have? How do you plan to develop those you don't yet have?

Of course, not all leaders are equal. Unfortunately, true leaders are few. Here are some of the attributes of true leaders:

- **Self-aware.** They know who they are and their uniqueness. They also recognize their imperfections. As much as they are aware of their strengths and what makes them tick, they also acknowledge their limitations. Because of that, they lead out of humility, believing that they need the support of others to complement them and to overcome these weaknesses.

- **Servant.** They put the needs and aspirations of others ahead of their own. They create an environment that allows others to meet their individual and corporate goals.
- **Resourceful.** They go beyond their backyard to attract talent, opportunities, and resources.
- **Resilient.** They don't easily give up. They endure and outlast setbacks.
- **Trustworthy.** Not only do they have the right attitude and mastery of their craft, but they also have a solid character. They have integrity that earns them trustworthiness.

Developing the above attributes of true leaders enables you to overcome and go beyond first-timer syndrome. Though discussing these attributes in detail is beyond the scope of this book, I must point out that true leadership demands working on one's character. One of the most common and universal character attributes, which is also mentioned above, is trustworthiness. Trustworthy leaders are predictable. Having clarity on one's leadership philosophy, communicating it, and demonstrating a commitment to live up to one's philosophy is the foundation of trustworthiness. It may take you years, if not decades, to develop and refine your character. However, the journey to become one of the great leaders in your field should begin now. A good starting place to work on your character is to lay the foundation by clarifying your philosophies.

9.2. The importance of leadership philosophy

As I said earlier, true leaders are self-aware. They know who they are, their values, what is expected of them, and what they expect from others. Have you worked for such a leader who had a leadership philosophy? Remember, some leaders don't call it a philosophy. Some may not write it down. But you can tell whether they have one or not based on their consistency and predictability.

Leadership philosophy determines how you:
- Think
- Behave
- Communicate and interact
- Decide and act
- Handle circumstances
- Respond to events

Whether you're aware of it or not, you have a leadership philosophy. It is your mental framework. It is the lens through which you see things.

If you haven't been conscious of your leadership philosophy and have never written it down, the following benefits may convince you to do so. With your leadership philosophy handy, you:
- Reveal to the people who work with you who you are and what matters the most to you

- Disclose your expectations and what you expect from others from the start
- Set the tone on how you will lead
- Become predictable, which is a good thing

9.3. Crafting your leadership philosophy

Once you're convinced about the need to have one, you should articulate your leadership philosophy. Bring it from your unconscious to your conscious mind. To help you articulate it, answer these questions:

a) **What is your leadership style?** What you believe about leadership dictates your style(s). What are three things you believe about leadership? What kind of a leader do you want to be? What kind(s) of style(s) could represent who you are?

b) **What are your top values?** What are three things that matter the most to you? What are three things you consider non-negotiable?

c) **What are your standards?** What are the bare minimums you expect from people who work with you? What are the core principles that you want your people to respect? How do you prefer them to interact with you? How can they add value to you and the team?

d) **What are your promises?** What will be your contributions to the relationship? What should people expect from you? How do they benefit from your leadership?

9.4. Communicating your leadership philosophy

Try to make your leadership philosophy a one-pager. Once you have the draft, communicate it with the people close to you to get their feedback. If you don't yet feel comfortable sharing it with your team or your manager, take your time. Continue to refine it until you feel confident about it.

Once you have the final version, communicate it with the people who work with you. You can use team meetings and one-on-ones to communicate it. Periodically, impart your leadership philosophy, especially for those who don't yet know you.

You should have a copy of it handy so you can share it whenever the opportunity presents itself. Of course, you can also put it online and share the link. Continue to improve it in the coming weeks and months. You will likely develop multiple versions of it over the years.

However, don't forget that coming up with your leadership philosophy and setting expectations from the get-go isn't enough. Yes, it quickens your ability to overcome first-timer syndrome and establish yourself as your team leader, but you must still demonstrate authenticity and remain credible by living up to your beliefs and values. The antidote in this chapter will eliminate any inconsistencies that might paint your trustworthiness and predictability in a negative light. The next antidote will treat inauthenticity or credibility issues.

ANTIDOTE 10

Become Authentic and Credible

"Authenticity is a collection of choices that we have to make every day. It's about the choice to show up and be real. The choice to be honest. The choice to let our true selves be seen."

Brene Brown, Professor, lecturer,
author, and podcast host.

In the previous chapter, you learned the need to articulate and share your leadership philosophy. It is my hope that you have begun crafting your leadership philosophy to join those elite leaders who articulate and regularly update their governing leadership principles. However, coming up with your leadership philosophy and setting expectations concerning your leadership style from the start is one thing, but demonstrating authenticity and remaining credible by living up to your beliefs and values is totally very different thing.

Many leadership experts agree that character is the glue of leadership. You may have plenty of great qualities but without character and a predictable personality, you won't command influence or a following, especially when you are the new kid on the block. Even if you have temporary influence because of your charisma and competencies, you will not keep it for long unless you have a solid character.

Of course, character is different for different people. From industry to industry, the character expectations of organizations vary. In this primer, I'm not going to dive deep. I also refrain from prescribing the kind of character attributes one should have. Instead, my goal is to bring your attention to the importance of developing a personality that boosts your influence from the get-go, even if many of the stakeholders may not yet know and trust you. I will also share with you some of the universal characters attributes that you should consider developing and refining while you're still an emerging leader.

One such universal character attribute of leadership is integrity. Former US President and military general who led the allied forces on D-Day in 1944, Dwight D. Eisenhower, said: **"The supreme quality of leadership is integrity."** Leaders with integrity are authentic and credible, and in return, influence their people with ease.

Though you need your solid character day in and day out, you need it even more when you face challenges and setbacks, which you will certainly have as a first-timer. These challenges and setbacks will test your character and let people know what you're made of. People are less interested in the kinds of problems, failures, and defeats you are experiencing. They are more interested in how you react. Did you quit or persist? Did you outlast the setbacks, did you give up quickly, or did you blame others?

You can lay the foundation for a solid character from the start by staying true to who you are and by remaining committed to your ideals and goals, regardless of the setbacks you experience in your first leadership role. That is why one of the great leaders of the 20th Century, Winston Churchill, observed: **"Success is not final, failure is not fatal: it is the courage to continue that counts."** One cannot muster courage without having a well-developed character. Only leaders with solid character stay put and stay on course, regardless of setbacks.

Character in general and authenticity and credibility, in particular, are crucial for first-timers. These smooth your transition. They enable you to quickly overcome first-timer syndrome. Authenticity and credibility are foundational for character. A leader without character, senior or novice, is a house built on shaky ground with a feeble foundation that cracks when a storm hits. As a first-timer, you have already been hit and will continue to be hit with storms.

Though developing the right mindset and skillsets are very helpful to succeed as a first-timer leader, your solid personality sustains you as you move through the transition period. This antidote in Chapter 10 empowers you to demonstrate authenticity and credibility. In addition, it equips you with the necessary strategies to take your character to the next level. When that happens, you can easily become likable and generate trust quickly.

I'm sure you have worked with inauthentic leaders. How did it feel to work for or with such leaders? You might also have worked with a leader you couldn't trust. What was it like to work for this leader? I don't think you would like to start your leadership like these leaders. Remember, many of the stakeholders don't know you yet and might reach wrong conclusions and assume that you're inauthentic and not credible. If there are any signs that could lead people to misjudge your character, this antidote will remedy them.

Diagnostic questions

- Have people questioned your trustworthiness even if you know that you are trustworthy and have the best interests of your people in mind?
- Has anyone in the past implied that you were unfair? Have you ever been accused of, even if wrongly, being inconsistent?
- Does some part within you worry that you're inauthentic?
- Have you been perceived as a 'know-it-all'?

If you answered yes to one or more of the above diagnostic questions, you're in the right chapter. This antidote takes away those factors that may predispose you to being perceived as inauthentic and not credible.

Learning Objectives

The main goal of this chapter is to enable you to increase your influence by becoming authentic and credible. Below are the specific objectives:

- To recognize the place of authenticity and credibility in leadership,
- To become authentic and credible,
- To practice consistency and fairness in order to generate trust,
- To become teachable through learning from your mistakes and by being vulnerable.

10.1. The place of authenticity and credibility

Among some of the most important character attributes one needs to be a true and impactful leader are authenticity and credibility. Almost everyone thinks they are trustworthy. They only question the integrity of others they don't yet know. They don't believe that they need to earn others' trust but expect others to trust them without providing reasons to be trusted. This inclination of others calls for your attention. You should be proactive in earning the trust of others by demonstrating authenticity and credibility, which will accelerate your smooth transition.

Here are some of the most important benefits of working on your character and developing an authentic and credible personality from the start. People:

- **Predict you.** Though they may not yet like you and agree with you, if they know that you're authentic and credible, people can easily predict your behavior and are willing to take the risk to work with you and follow your lead. They know how you will behave going forward.

- **Trust you.** Working with someone you don't trust is like going out to battle without that person having your back. If you have such a leader, you won't follow him or her wholeheartedly. The author of The 7 Habits of Highly Effective People, Steven Covey said it well: **"Trust is the glue of life. It's the most essential ingredient in effective communication. It's the foundational principle that holds all relationships."** Your people trust you when they see that you are authentic and credible, and thus, they are willing to go far with you even if you're full of flaws and incompetency.

- **Give their best.** When people are led by someone who is authentic and credible, they give their best. They won't have reservations. They go all in.

As an emerging leader, you need these benefits to thrive beyond first-time leadership pitfalls. The quicker you become authentic and credible as a first-timer, the faster you will move beyond first-timer syndrome.

Nonetheless, don't forget that building a solid character takes time and consistency. Wherever you may be right now, shorten becoming authentic and credible by taking the antidote in this chapter.

10.2. Become authentic and credible

By now, you may be convinced about the place of character in general and authenticity and credibility in particular. However, it is not enough to understand their place. You should begin developing some of the most crucial character elements from day one. Of course, you will continue to work on other character attributes as you advance in your leadership. But, at this stage, you should at least become authentic and credible in the eyes of the people you work with.

Authenticity is about expressing yourself without contradictions. When your inner world and how you present yourself to the outside world are aligned, you are authentic. I can tell you this. Most of us don't think we are inauthentic. Still, even if we think we are authentic, others may not perceive us so. That's why we're here, to become intentional so that others will see your authenticity.

People are watching you all the time, even if they or you are not conscious of it. They are taking mental notes even if they do not tell you to your face. They analyze you and make conclusions they may not even be aware of. But of course their conclusions could be wrong. Sadly, there is nothing you can do about that.

Chris Argyris, business theorist and professor emeritus at Harvard Business School, came up with a concept called 'Ladder of Inference,' which explains the above phenomenon. We all infer, and all the time. Very few of us are conscious of many of our inferences and the rest of us are almost completely unaware. We run the virtual ladder without even knowing we are on a 'ladder' multiple times every day. You see someone or something, and you run up your ladder. We all do it.

When we run the ladder, our brain is helping us be smart, quick, and safe. Yes, there are times when we need such shortcuts. But first we should pause and climb down the ladder to see if we're missing some valuable data that could help us make more accurate, wise, and ethical decisions.

Here is the science behind how inference works:

- We **gather data** through our sense organs and send it to the brain via the spinal cord
- Our brain uses the database that already exists in our long-term memory to **authenticate the new data** we just gathered
- The brain then **adds meaning** to the new data
- Based on the meaning, the brain **comes up with assumptions**. But since we only focus on those data aligned with our existing beliefs, in spite of the comprehensive data in front of us, we have knowledge gaps, so some of these assumptions may be wrong.

- The brain **concludes** and suggests a course of action. This can happen within seconds and without our conscious involvement.

The problem is that you don't see what is running in the heads of others. They, too, may not be aware. The frustrating thing is that their conclusion about you could be wrong because of wrong assumptions. They may think that you are inauthentic and might exhibit behaviors and actions that suggest to you that they don't trust you. But you cannot challenge their conclusions or actions. If you try, they resist and further reinforce their unconscious mistrust.

Here are a couple of things you can do to overcome this challenge:

- Bring others down the ladder by asking questions. When you encounter people who quickly run the virtual ladder up and reach wrong conclusions, you should engage with them in conversation. Say, for instance, 'I see that you don't want to share your data with my team.' They most probably reveal to you their conclusions- why they don't trust your team. This approach is better than directly confronting and telling others why they don't trust your team. Challenging their conclusions doesn't take you anywhere.

- Once you know their conclusion, you will have a better chance to have follow-up questions to understand other people's assumptions. Once you uncover the wrong assumptions they have, you will be able to determine their knowledge gaps and will know which data they didn't gather.

- You can then offer data that might cause them to reverse their assumptions and, as a result, their conclusions. This will allow you to gain their trust as well as the data your team needs.

The above steps are meant for when you find out that people 'believe' that you or your team are not credible. But instead of waiting until they question your authenticity and credibility, be proactive. Be sure to provide enough data for them to form the correct assumptions and reach conclusions in your favor.

10.3. Practice consistency and fairness

The more you become consistent in your words, behaviors, and actions, the more your people find you authentic. Unfortunately, below are some of the things that may create inconsistency and rob you of your authenticity:

- **Compartmentalized life**. If you behave and act differently in the office than you do outside the office.
- **Double-faced communication.** This is when you say something in private but something else publicly.
- **Conformity.** When you stop living up to your beliefs and values because of fear of rejection, to appease others or to avoid unwanted consequences.
- **Broken promises.** When you break your promises and hide rather than apologize or renegotiate.

The fairer your decisions are, the more people find you credible. Even if they don't agree with you or even like you, they respect your decisions. They understand that you have a known and fair process you use to make decisions. They may not like your choices at all, but at least they know that you have the best interests of your people and the organization in your heart.

The more credible you become, the more people trust you and want to work with you. And the more they trust you, the more you can work with them. In his book, *The Speed of Trust*, Stephen M. R. Covey talks about how when trust is high, things are done fast, while when trust is low, things are done slowly, costing time and resources.

Here are some areas where you can demonstrate consistency:

- Be consistent in your communication, both verbal and non-verbal.
- Let your behaviors and manners be consistent with what you believe and state in public.
- Make sure your actions aren't contradicting your words, promises, and deeds.

Be consistent in your communication

Let's just expand on the first area right now. How can you engage in consistent communication? Here are some suggestions:

- Let your voice back your words. If you say you are excited, let your voice show that you're truly excited.

- Develop mindfulness, so that you are paying attention to the behaviors and manners you manifest consistently. There shouldn't be a time where you let loose, since that could lead to people questioning your authenticity. Of course, I'm not suggesting that you be tight and vigilant all the time. If you are authentic, there should be no need to police yourself.

You need to be mindful of any inconsistencies that may manifest. And even if you fall from grace occasionally, there is no need to panic. Take lessons and work on your personality and character to address the misstep. No one is perfect all the time, and you're no exception. Most people will understand unless you make things worse by trying to cover it up or deny it.

- Prepare for each talk you have, whether formal, informal, one-on-one or to a large group. Don't wing it. As you prepare and rehearse, some inconsistencies may surface. Do the same when you communicate virtually and over the phone, especially with people you don't yet have a rapport with.
- Re-read emails before sending them, especially when you are communicating with people who may not yet know you very well.

Exhibit fairness

Fairness is part of having a solid character. As a first-timer, to become and remain credible, you should be fair by doing the following:

1. Treat everyone equally, as fellow human beings
   - Regardless of their performance,
   - Whether you like them or not,
   - During their ups and downs.

2. Share your authority. Though you're authorized to lead, share your authority by
   - Being participatory in your decisions,
   - Deferring some of the decisions to the team,
   - Delegating some decisions.

3. Show mercy when you make decisions that affect others. You can show compassion even if you have to confront and address issues caused by some of your team members. Show mercy by
   - Giving second chances,
   - Avoiding penalizing unless you have no other course of action,
   - Being soft on the people but hard on the issue.
     Think about a time where you were mistreated because you stumbled. What did you feel? Think again about when you felt you were given some slack even if you didn't deserve it. How did you react? With which person would you love to work? It's obvious! Going forward, how do you want to treat your people when they stumble?

10.4. Be teachable and vulnerable

Becoming authentic and credible as much as possible doesn't mean you have to be perfect. Nobody is perfect, and no one can become perfect. However, we all need to grow toward perfection, even if we may not attain it during our lifetime.

This is especially true for first-timers. It is okay to be vulnerable and teachable in your current leadership position. No one should judge you if you open up and express your struggles and ask for help. You may be surprised to find out that people are eager to help you and show you the ropes when you become teachable and vulnerable.

It is somewhat risky to appear invulnerable. People quickly label you as someone who is naïve and who doesn't even know what you don't know. Trying to seem invulnerable paints you as inauthentic and less credible.

Here are a couple of things you should be mindful of as you present yourself as teachable. These things will increase your chance of winning other people's help:

- **Show that you are a learner.** Ask questions, and be curious.
- **Be willing to ask for help.** When you struggle to understand, admit it. When you are doubtful, afraid, concerned, etc., express these feelings. Don't worry, this doesn't contradict what I advised you in Chapter 2, where I encouraged you to own your place and be assertive. You can still be in charge and confident

while being vulnerable in areas where you need help. This makes you authentic, not weak.

- **Admit mistakes without delay.** We all make mistakes. Only inauthentic people struggle to admit they committed an error, which erodes their credibility.

Critically assess your attitude to see if there are signs that you're unteachable and arrogant. Here are some attitudes you should avoid:

- I know it all
- I've got it all together
- I am superhuman
- I don't need help
- I'm perfect
- I'm invincible
- I'm untouchable

Since you're reading this book, I suspect you don't possess any of the above attitudes, at least as far as you're aware. But you may *appear* arrogant and unteachable unless you're careful and intentional. Deep inside, you might be humble, but people may not be able to see it on the outside. That is why you must be vulnerable.

Vulnerability is a relatively new concept in leadership. We have been taught not to be vulnerable, and being vulnerable as a leader has been painted as being weak. As a result, leaders feel uncomfortable sharing their struggles and limitations. If this is a new thing for you and you are not yet convinced, take it slowly. Think and reflect to find those initial places where you may want to be vulnerable.

Thanks to Brene Brown, the author of Dare to Lead, vulnerability has now been given the attention it deserves. She clarified, **"Vulnerability is not winning or losing; it's having the courage to show up and be seen when we have no control over the outcome."** This kind of courage is crucial to be credible in the 21ˢᵗ Century. More and more leaders have begun to realize that we all have areas in which we struggle, and where things do not always go well for us.

If we attempt to fake it and pretend that we are superhuman and are without vulnerability, we lose our authenticity and credibility. To be clear, vulnerability doesn't mean you have to share every 'wound' (hurts, disappointments, rejections, etc.) you've received. Some wounds need to heal first, for your and others' sake, before you expose them. They may not heal, or the healing process may be protracted. Work on such wounds and hurts, and let them heal and only then share your scars.

ANTIDOTE 11

Develop Yourself and Your People

"The growth and development of people is the highest calling of leadership."

Harvey S. Firestone,
Founder of the Firestone Tire
and Rubber Company.

The previous chapter emphasized the need to be an authentic leader with credibility from the get-go. You learned the important role character plays in leadership. No one can become a true and successful leader without developing a solid character. Influencing others and commanding a following, especially as an emerging leader, demands intentional character-building by demonstrating consistency, exhibiting fairness, and being teachable.

The previous antidote empowered you to be consistent in your communications, behaviors, decisions, and actions. It equipped you to demonstrate fairness, share your authority, and show grace and mercy for those who may need it once in a while. These bare minimum character attributes should enable you to withstand first-timer syndrome and accelerate your ability to overcome it. It will help if you realize that character development isn't a one-time endeavor, and that the previous two chapters aren't enough. Yes, you should grow in your mindset and skill set throughout your leadership. Growth in your character set, nonetheless, is going to be a lifetime assignment. As first lady Eleanor Roosevelt said, **"*Character* building begins in our infancy and continues until death."**

By now, you may already suspect that you were not promoted because you were perfect for the position or because there was no one else who could have been promoted instead. This reality should humble you to work on yourself by growing intentionally, beginning now.

The antidote in this final chapter is going to stretch and challenge you to grow yourself and your people intentionally in those areas you need the most as you go beyond the syndrome to thrive in your first-time leadership position. This antidote empowers you to raise the bar high and maintain your and your team's growth to prevent relapse of the syndrome. How quickly you can overcome the syndrome is directly proportionate to your willingness to grow. Your success beyond the first-timer syndrome is also dependent on your dedication to empowering your team. As John C. Maxwell underscored: **"The single biggest way to impact an organization is to focus on**

leadership development. There is almost no limit to the potential of an organization that recruits good people, raises them as leaders, and continually develops them."

Unfortunately, many emerging leaders are unaware of one crucial reality. They know that we have to be deliberate about our physical growth by eating and exercising right and regularly. But they don't give the same deliberate attention to leadership growth. They may not yet take these sayings seriously: 'Leaders are learners' and 'Leaders are readers.' They might not have heard what journalist and women's rights activist- Margaret Fuller said: **"Today a reader, tomorrow a leader."** Remember, on top of overcoming the first-timer syndrome, your long-term success depends on your and your people's growth. Successful leaders regularly invest in themselves and also grow their people.

Most of the antidotes so far cannot be effective and lasting with only one dose. You must take multiple doses, especially of those antidotes you need the most. If you desire to thrive beyond first-time leadership pitfalls, you have to learn and grow consistently long after finishing this book.

Even if you feel good about where you are right now, and no matter how well things are going for you, you should continue to learn and expand. You should feel uncomfortable about where you are right now. If you are comfortable, you are less likely to stretch yourself. It is also unlikely you will set an example to stretch and help your team grow.

Diagnostic questions
- Do you or your team have challenging problems that are slowing you down?
- Have you or your team struggled to meet your goals?
- Do you lack a leadership development plan for yourself and your team?
- Do you have team members who are struggling to perform?

If one or more of these is true, you need this antidote. First, you need quick holistic growth, both personally and in your business.

Learning Objectives

The main goal of this chapter is to inspire you to prioritize continual leadership growth and offer you some guidance to develop yourself and your people. Below are the specific objectives:
- To emphasize the vital place of holistic and continual growth in leadership
- To provide frameworks to develop yourself and your people
- To intentionally help your vulnerable team members grow

11.1. The vital roles of holistic growth

Why should you take leadership growth seriously? Leadership works inside out. Unless a leader grows within, there is nothing significant the leader can achieve on the outside. Thus, leadership is an inside job.

When you study impactful leaders, you will learn that they constantly grow. Not only that, they grow holistically. They are intentional about their growth in the different aspects of their leadership. As a result, they experience all-around improvements.

The moment a leader stops growing, they risk stagnation. If they don't address it quickly, it leads to irrelevance. Though one's title and authority may give a leader formal leverage over the people she is assigned to lead, people follow someone they respect and admire. There is nothing to admire and respect about stagnation and irrelevance. And without the former, it will be hard for an emerging leader to go beyond the first-timer syndrome and thrive in her new leadership role.

The growth I'm talking about is holistic. I've noticed that many leaders grow in a few aspects of their leadership, while neglecting other areas. What is challenging is that holistic growth is not a one-time endeavor. It is a continual process that demands serious commitment, and a process that you should begin immediately. Mahatma Gandhi once said, **"I live as if I die tomorrow, and learn as if I live forever."** What a healthy perspective about growth!

If you don't grow, your perspectives, outlooks, understanding, patience, wisdom, and so on don't grow. On the other hand, when you remain at one level, your results and influence remain there too. On top of that, people around you realize that you're remaining at one level. What happens to a shepherd whose sheep discover that he is no longer up to the task of leading the herd? They begin to 'look' for another shepherd or 'stop trusting and following' the existing shepherd. This should all motivate you to invest in your growth.

11.2. Develop yourself

You might have worked for or with a stagnant leader. What was it like? How did it impact you and the team? I'm sure it didn't go well.

I've had a few leaders who neglected their growth. I knew it because they lacked freshness. They said the same things again and again; shared the same old stories and examples. They no longer challenged me. They were unable to stretch me or other team members, and we all talked about it.

The challenge of leadership growth is that many leaders don't think they need it. They assume that they have what it takes. What they don't understand is that when they were promoted, they were given the position on credit, with the hope that they would meet the demands of the position and ultimately outgrow it.

Even those leaders who are committed to growing may not grow holistically. Part of the reason is that they may unconsciously think they have arrived. I hope that your recent promotion won't lead you to think like these leaders. To avoid stagnation, you must have a growth mindset.

I will admit that growing yourself consistently requires being intentional. You must dedicate your scarce resources, as well as strategize, prioritize, monitor, and evaluate your progress. You should also develop a growth habit. Once this habit is formed, your growth journey becomes more effortless.

To overcome first-timer syndrome using holistic growth, you should:

- Identify areas where you may need immediate growth,
- Create a comprehensive development plan,
- Execute your plan faithfully, and
- Evaluate your progress and make adjustments.

a) Identify areas for your growth

We all have specific areas we need to grow, and you're no exception. Identify those particular areas where you need to grow. Overall, you may need to grow in these three major leadership growth areas:

- **Mindset.** Where are you when it comes to your attitude? Is your attitude assisting you to overcome first-timer syndrome or is it getting in the way? Do you have the 'I can change' mindset, which is necessary to go beyond first-time leadership pitfalls? Do you have a growth mindset?
- **Skill-set.** Which leadership skills do you need the most to make a smooth transition? Among the competencies we have covered so far, which ones need further work to excel in your current leadership

role? For which critical skills do you need training and coaching?

- **Character-set.** Where does your character stand? Which character attributes need work? Are you perceived as consistent and predictable? Have you generated trust by demonstrating authenticity and credibility? Do you have the influence you need to succeed as an emerging leader? Do you have resilience? Do you have endurance?

You might be very well developed in one of these three components of leadership but lagging in others. To overcome first-timer syndrome quickly, give primary focus to the area in which you feel most inadequate.

Don't get overwhelmed. You have many responsibilities, both at home and at work. Your plate is already full. Make sure to pick top areas of growth for the next 6 months. Once you grow in these areas, you can choose the next priority area(s).

b) Plan for your growth

Once you identify your growth area(s), develop strategies and tactics to improve them. For example, let's say you decided to increase your and your team's visibility. What are some strategies and tactics you can use to increase your visibility? I'll suggest one strategy and one tactic as an example, but you can pick multiple strategies and tactics for each development area.

Strategy: You may choose a strategy to express your opinion on the company's intranet site.

Tactic: One tactic could be posting short blogs on the intranet site. Another could be periodically reporting the achievements of your team.

c) Execute your plan

The most challenging part is executing your well-developed development plan. Here are a couple of things you might do to improve your execution:

- Break down large tasks into smaller and more manageable tasks.
- Make sure to put the specific tasks on your calendar, and discipline yourself to execute one task at a time.
- You might wish to use some platforms, such as Outlook, to automate and receive notifications.
- Consider allocating some resources and backup plans in case things don't go as you hope.
- Protect your schedule. Learn how to say no to protect your top priorities.

d) Evaluate

You have to consistently monitor and evaluate your progress. Things may not go the way you anticipate. When that happens, you may need to invoke your backup plan.

Evaluate your progress. When necessary, take corrective actions. For instance, if you don't see major changes using your strategies and tactics, consider finding a coach(es) and mentor(s).

Of course, if you have the option, you should have coaches and mentors even if you are showing progress in your growth plan. They help you make yourself accountable for your own growth goals. They can stretch you and share insights, models, tools, strategies, and tactics that will help you move to the next level quicker, and in turn, beat first-timer syndrome fast. You can stand on their shoulders to see far. You can learn from their successes and duplicate those things with some customization and also avoid repeating the mistakes they have made.

11.3. Develop your team

On top of growing yourself, you have to give growing your people the same attention in order to go beyond first-time leadership pitfalls. Jack Welch, former President and CEO of General Electric, said: "Before you are a leader, success is all about growing yourself. When you become a leader, success is all about growing others."

Here are some incentives that may motivate you to develop your team:

- When you develop your team, you're responding to the highest calling of leadership. Here is what Harvey S. Firestone, founder of Firestone Tire and Rubber Company, believed: **"The growth and development of people is the highest calling of leadership."**
- You will become relevant in the 21ˢᵗ Century. Bill Gates, founder of Microsoft, acknowledged that **"As we look ahead into the next century, leaders will be those who empower others."**

- You will have a chance to multiply yourself. Former US President Ronald Reagan admitted: **"The greatest leader is not necessarily the one who does the greatest things. He is the one that gets the people to do the greatest things."**

If you're convinced that you should grow your people, the next question is how? Act as a coach! In the 21ˢᵗ Century, you can't just play boss. You should develop your coaching ability to help grow your team.

Then, ask these questions and get answers:

- Do they need growth in understanding the organization and its workings? If you recall, the first antidote was about knowing your place. Do your people know their relative place in the organization and on the team?
- Do they have the right attitude? Do they believe in themselves and in their fellow team members? Do they have the confidence to do the job and overcome any challenge they may face, whether individually or collectively?
- What about their technical and soft skills? Which skills does the team or do individual members need to succeed?
- Do they lack any character attributes?

Based on your assessment above concerning growth areas for your team, select the top three agendas for each development area. Strategize and prioritize. Allocate resources. Come up with a plan just like the one you came up with for your personal growth. Put it on your team's calendar, and execute it faithfully. Monitor their progress and evaluate the effectiveness of the corporate growth plan, and make changes if necessary.

Of course, if you have the budget, you may send them offsite to attend additional training. You might invite trainers and coaches to support your efforts. Even if you don't get the approval and budget to use outside resources to grow your people, you should try your best to help them grow in-house.

11.4. Grow your vulnerable team members

It is great that you are growing yourself and your team as a whole. However, you also need to give special attention to the vulnerable members. Jim Rohn, American entrepreneur, author and motivational speaker, articulated it very well: **"A good objective of leadership is to help those who are doing poorly to do well and to help those who are doing well to do even better."**

While stretching those team members to continue to perform by leveraging their strengths, you should give special attention to those who may be lagging to meet their performance goals and those who may have some soft (people) skills and character issues. The goal is to help those who are struggling to improve their performance and continue to outperform themselves. Be a great leader and heed the advice of Orrin Woodward, Founder and

Chairman of the Board of LIFE: **"Average leaders raise the bar on themselves; good leaders raise the bar for others; great leaders inspire others to raise their own bar."**

Here are the steps you should consider to transform vulnerable and struggling team members into top performers:

- Recognize vulnerable members of the team very early,
- Identify the areas where they struggle,
- Create a tailored development plan for each one,
- Put it on your and their calendar, execute, monitor, evaluate, and make changes if necessary.

Of course, leadership development, like any other growth, requires commitment and consistency. There is no shortcut, nor can you delegate it. You cannot say I worked on my development last week, and now let me take it easy and relax for the next three weeks or months. Your body doesn't grow unless you feed it quality food daily. Your body doesn't become strong and resilient without consistent exercise. Likewise, your leadership growth needs your consistent commitment by practicing what you learn and making changes when what you implement doesn't work.

Conclusion

My hat is off to you for reading this book in its entirety. Carving out time from your busy schedule to finish reading the book takes courage, dedication, and commitment. Many wouldn't care to read a book dedicated to first-timer leaders. Others might pick it up but not finish it as you did. Thus, congrats!

That said, let me ask you a few closing questions:

- What are the top three key lessons you have learned from this book?
- What are your top three antidotes that contributed the most to overcome your first-timer syndrome?
- What three immediate actions will you take as a result of reading this book that will enable you to thrive beyond first-time leadership pitfalls?
- Now that you've finished the book, you will likely soon be making a smooth transition. So how might you keep the momentum going and continue to build on what you have already built?

I'd love to hear your answers to these questions. Please use either one of my email addresses below to share your responses with me. If you give me permission, I would like to share them on my website, so that others may learn from you.

By reading this book, you have prepared yourself to overcome first-timer syndrome very quickly. I hope that from now on you will assist other first-timers in your organization to experience a smooth transition in their first-time leadership roles. I also believe that the insights, tools, strategies, and tactics you learned in this book will empower you to succeed outside of work; at home, in your neighborhood, and in the marketplace.

It was a pleasure for me to be your cheerleader throughout this book. However, I don't want to relinquish this role simply because you've finished reading it. I would like to encourage you to continue reviewing what you have learned here.

Research shows that we forget the lion's sharing of what we learn unless we review and take actions based on the learning. Therefore, for the next four weeks, make sure to go back and read the notes you have taken. More than anything else, take some actions that allow you to develop certain competencies and essential habits. I encourage you to go out and rock it!

Remember, leadership ends in death. You will never retire from leadership. As John F. Kennedy said: **"Leadership and learning are indispensable to each other."** This journey of learning you have taken by reading this book is a start. You should continue to grow. Attend more live and online courses. By all means, don't ever stop growing.

If you choose me as your cheerleader and virtual coach as you continue to grow as an emerging leader, below are the programs for you to consider for yourself or for fellow emerging leaders:

- Online course to overcome first-timer syndrome in leadership
- One-on-one or group coaching
- Emerging Leaders Program
- You can also invite me to speak at your future events based on one of the themes covered in the book.

We also offer other complementary programs that will empower you in your current and future leadership positions. In addition, we will soon be making available similar books for first-timer mid-level managers and executives. As you transition into the mid-level manager and executive leadership positions, you will find these books invaluable to make a smooth transition. You can use them as manuals to guide your first-timer journey as a manager and then an executive. Stay tuned!

Below is my contact info.
Reach out if you may have any questions.

P.O. Box 10136
Silver Spring, MD 20914

Email: Assegid@successpws.com or
Assegidh@gmail.com

Tel: 703-895-4551

Printed in Great Britain
by Amazon

67906569R00122